Lester Barenbaum
Walter Schubert
Robert Feder

The Family Lawyer's Guide to

Stock Options

AMERICAN BAR ASSOCIATION
Defending Liberty
Pursuing Justice

SECTION OF
FAMILY LAW

Cover design by ABA Publishing

Printed in the United States of America

12   5 4 3 2

Cataloging-in-Publication data is on file with the Library of Congress

Family lawyer's guide to stock options / Barenbaum, Lester, Schubert, Walter, Feder, Robert
    ISBN: 1-59031-790-4

Contents

About the Authors

Lester Barenbaum is a Managing Director of Financial Research Associates, a litigation support firm located outside Philadelphia, Pennsylvania. Dr. Barenbaum has testified as an expert witness on the valuation of employee stock options and on the value of closely held firms. He also is a Full Professor of Finance at LaSalle University where he teaches graduate Finance.

Walter Schubert is a Full Professor of Finance at La Salle University in Philadelphia, Pennsylvania, where he has published several articles dealing with value of employee stock options. Dr. Schubert is often an invited speaker at both regional and national valuation conferences.

Robert Feder is a partner at Schnader Harrison Segal & Lewis, LLP. He specializes in family law. He is the co-author of several texts dealing with equitable distribution and he has appeared on both television and radio to discuss current issues in family law.

Acknowledgments

The authors would like to thank their colleagues for the invaluable feedback and support for this project.

Glossary

Alternative Minimum Tax (AMT): The AMT was introduced in 1969. It uses a different system of rules for determining taxable income. The gain from exercising employee stock options may result in individuals paying greater taxes under the normal tax code.

At-the-Money Stock Option: An option where the exercise price of an option equals the share price of the underlying security. An at-the-money stock option has a zero intrinsic value.

Black-Scholes Options Price Model (BSOPM): A mathematical model used to determine the value of traded and employee stock options. The model incorporates factors such as the intrinsic value of the option, the expected level of risk free rates, the expected holding period for the option, the expected dividend yield of the underlying security, and an estimate of expected volatility of future stock returns of the underlying security. The Black-Scholes Option Pricing Model is known as a closed-form model.

Binomial Option Pricing Model: A mathematical model used to determine the value of stock options. The binomial model is an open-form model that allows greater flexibility in assumptions than the Black-Scholes. For example, under the binomial model one can specify early exercise in terms of holding period and the ratio of share price to exercise price.

Cashless Exercise: When the exercise of employee stock options is accomplished by using shares of stock sold upon exercise to meet the exercise cost.

Collar: A combination of calls and puts that allows an investor to minimize marketability risk.

Coverture Ratio: A ratio designed to determine the proportion of option value subject to equitable distribution. It is generally employed when an employee stock option vests after the date joint marital efforts end. A typical coverture ratio takes the following form:

$$\frac{\text{Date at which service began} - \text{Date at which marital efforts end}}{\text{Date at which service began} - \text{Date at which the option vests}}$$

Dividend Yield: The annual dollar dividend a stock pays into the share price of the security. The stock option holder forfeits the dividend yield when investing in options relative to direct purchases of stock. Consequently, the dividend yield of a common stock reduces the value of an option.

Exercise Price (Call Option): The price at which the underlying security can be purchased. Also called the strike price.

Expiration Date: The last date on which an option holder may exercise the option. This date usually is set forth in the option award letter.

Employee Stock Option: A stock option that is part of an employee's compensation package. They are always call options— that is, they provide the employee the right but not the obligation to purchase the underlying security at a fixed price for a fixed time frame. They differ from traded options in that they generally are not transferable and typically have a longer life than traded options.

Expected Holding Period: The expected time remaining before an option will be exercised. Generally, employee stock options have an expected holding period less than the time to expiration.

Fair Value: The price at which an employee stock option can be bought or sold in an open market transaction. Generally accepted accounting principles (GAAP) now require firms to estimate and disclose the fair value of employee stock options they have granted. The disclosure is required for both vested and unvested options.

Grant Date: The date an employee stock option is awarded to an employee. The award creates a contingent asset for the employee.

Intrinsic Value: The difference between the market price of a security and the exercise price of an option. The intrinsic value cannot be negative. At any point in time, the intrinsic value represents the pre-tax liquidation value of an option.

In-the-Money Stock Option: An option where the exercise price of the option is less than the share price of the underlying security. In-the-money stock options have a positive intrinsic value.

Incentive Stock Option (Qualified Stock Option or Statutory Stock Option): When an employee stock option grant qualifies for certain federal tax benefits, it is classified as an incentive stock option. The major tax benefit is the delay in a taxable event until the underlying security received is sold. Furthermore, the gain from selling the underlying security will be treated as a long-term capital gain.

Nonqualified Stock Option (Nonstatutory Stock Option): When an employee stock option does not qualify as an incentive stock option, it is called a nonqualified stock option. Recognition of taxable income occurs when the option is exercised.

Performance Stock Option: Performance stock options often have vesting conditions that depend upon firm performance rather than time. Division profitability or revenue growth are typical performance metrics that trigger vesting.

Open Interest: The volume of options held by investors at a point in time.

Out-of-the-Money Stock Option: An option that is out of the money has an exercise price that is greater than the underlying share price. The intrinsic value of such an option is zero. Out-of-the-money stock options are often called underwater options.

Reload Option: An option that automatically grants new options when existing options are exercised. Reload options are not very common. When reload options are granted post separation from options that were marital, the reload option may have a marital component.

Restricted Stock: Stock that cannot be sold in the open market.

Risk-Free Rate: A risk-free rate normally refers to the yield of government securities without default risk. Yields on risk-free instruments with the same duration as the expected holding period are used in option pricing models.

Stock Appreciation Rights (SAR): A SAR allows the holder to benefit from the appreciation in an underlying security. Similar to employee stock options.

Stock Option (Call): A financial instrument that provides the right but not the obligation to purchase shares of stock at a fixed price (exercise price) for a finite time period.

Stock Option (Put): A financial instrument that provides one the right but not the obligation to sell shares of stock at a fixed price (exercise price) for a finite time period.

Time Value: The component of option value beyond the option's intrinsic value. The time value of an option represents value created by an option's right but not the obligation to purchase shares of stock at a fixed price for a finite time period.

Volatility: The fluctuations in security returns over time. Volatility typically is measured by the standard deviation of security returns. Greater volatility increases the value of a stock option.

Vesting Date: The date an employee receives title to an employee stock option through the option's expiration date. Option vesting can be based upon a graded schedule, such as 25% of options granted vest each year. Option vesting can also follow a cliff vesting schedule where all options vest after a certain time period. Alternatively, performance options vest after some goal is reached, such as a division's profit margin.

Introduction

Over 14 million American workers now receive employee stock options, an increase from one million in 1990.[1] Further, 79% of stock option holders earn less than $75,000 annually. Now that stock options have become a dominant component of compensation for both senior executives and middle management in public companies, the treatment of employee stock options has become of even greater importance for matrimonial attorneys.

Employee stock options generally are not transferable and thus represent nontraded assets. Consequently, their "value" is difficult to ascertain and, in many cases, is not realizable at the valuation date used for property. Furthermore, in many situations, employee stock options may have been granted prior to the date of the divorce complaint, but the employee will not receive full title (or vest) unless the employee continues employment with the firm beyond the complaint date. Thus, determining what component of executive stock options, if any, represents marital property for distribution is a difficult issue to resolve. How child support is impacted by the granting and subsequent exercise of employee stock options also is a topic that presents many questions requiring careful analysis. For example, how does the timing of the exercise of employee stock options impact the level of child support?

This manual provides guidance in answering these and other important questions. What follows is a brief overview of each of the five chapters comprising this guide to employee stock options. We hope that you find the material useful, timely, and clear.

Chapter 1: When Are Employee Stock Options Marital Property?
Chapter 1 is divided into three sections. The first section discusses why employee stock options generally are considered property. The second section addresses the complex issue of whether unvested employee stock options should be considered marital property and is discussed through a review of major court decisions around the coun-

try. Unvested stock options generally are viewed as a contingent asset because the employee-spouse does not have the right to exercise the stock option until vesting. The third section examines the various "time rules" typically used to allocate employee stock options between marital and separate property. Appendix 1-A contains a summary of major court cases addressing whether employee stock options represent marital property. Appendix 1-B provides a discovery checklist of items to request when assessing whether employee stock options represent marital property. Both appendices are available on the accompanying CD-ROM for easy customization. Chapter highlights include:

- Factors that help determine whether employee stock options were granted for past or future service;
- Examples of the various time-rule formulas to allocate unvested employee stock options into marital and separate property; and
- Language found in stock option plans that indicate why employee stock options have been granted.

Chapter 2: Employee Stock Option Valuation. Traded stock options have value by providing investors greater upside potential with limited downside risk relative to purchasing shares of the underlying security outright. Employee stock options also have these characteristics with two major differences. First, employee stock options generally are nontransferable. A major issue for family law attorneys is how this lack of marketability impacts both the value of employee stock options and their effective division in a property settlement.

Second, the term of employee stock options is significantly greater than that of traded stock options. As discussed in this chapter, this difference materially increases the value of employee stock options.

Chapter 2 is divided into three main sections. The first section provides an overview of stock option terminology and valuation using examples of traded stock options. The second section discusses how stock options are valued. The critical assumptions needed to value employee stock options are identified as well as how these assumptions can be validated. The chapter ends with an in-depth look at how employee stock option valuation differs from that of traded stock options. Key points pertaining to the valuation of employee stock as they relate to equitable distribution are listed below:

- Out-of-the-money traded and employee stock options often have significant value. For example, traded Apple Computer stock options with an exercise price $8.70 greater than the market price that expire in two years were trading at $19.00.
- Employee stock option value can be determined with reasonable accuracy. Generally accepted accounting principles now require firms to recognize the cost of options granted to employees determined through option pricing models such as the Black-Scholes Option Pricing Model directly on their income statement. The IRS mandates the use of the Black-Scholes Option Pricing Model for valuation of employee stock options in a gift and estate tax settings.
- The value of an employee stock option should be based upon the expected life of the option. The use of the contractual life of the option rather than the expected time to exercise will result in the option being overvalued.
- The reduction in the value of an employee stock option due to its lack of marketability is captured through reducing the expected life of the option. Using a shorter life and a marketability discount will understate the value of the option to the employee.
- A marketability discount may be appropriate if, after exercise, the employee has restrictions on sale of the underlying security. Discounts in the range of 5% to 15% are warranted.

Chapter 3: Taxation of Employee Stock Options, Restricted Stock, and Stock Appreciation Rights. Employee tax liability resulting from the exercise of employee stock options is an important factor that family law practitioners must address as part of any property settlement. Chapter 3 discusses how employee stock options are taxed with an emphasis on the differences between incentive stock options (qualified) and nonqualified employee stock options. New tax rulings dealing with employee stock options are discussed along with several examples of how they impact the net proceeds from the exercise of employee stock options.

Chapter 4: Deferred Distribution vs. Immediate Offset Approaches to Dividing Employee Stock Options. Once employee stock options are determined to be marital property and to have value, they must be distributed or divided. One of two methods of distribution typically is employed. The immediate offset approach to dividing employee stock options often is preferred by the titled spouse who believes his or her employee stock options may substantially grow in value. In addition, this approach creates a clean break between parties, unlike the deferred distribution approach, which requires the parties to maintain a working relationship. The facts and circumstances in any given situation will, of course, determine whether this method makes sense. The deferred distribution method, often referred to as the "if, as, and when approach" of dividing marital vested and unvested stock options, has been the court's preferred method. The advantage of this approach is that it eliminates the need to estimate the current value of unvested stock options. The advantages and disadvantages of this method are discussed. Because the vast majority of divorce cases settle out of court, stock options usually are distributed pursuant to the terms of a written agreement. A sample property settlement agreement is included as Appendix 4-A, and is also available on the accompanying CD-ROM.

Chapter 5: Stock Options as Income for Child Support and Alimony. How child support is impacted by the granting and subsequent exercise of employee stock options is a topic with many twists and turns. Vested employee stock options represent value to the option holder but may have no realizable value at the date of vesting. A deferral of the exercise date of employee stock options may provide the titled spouse the ability to reduce child support. Courts generally have considered vested options income upon exercise when they are converted into gross cash income or upon vesting when the ability to convert the option into income becomes possible. After an overview of the issues of when employee stock option income should be counted as part of gross income, a review of major court cases dealing with this issue is included. The chapter then moves on to a review of the use of a constructive trust to manage the use of employee stock options as part of child support. The listing of cases in Appendices 5-A and 5-B (also available on the accompanying CD-ROM) will assist attorneys in developing strategies in determining how employee stock options impact child support and alimony. Important issues discussed in the chapter include:

- Child support agreements should explicitly address how stock options will be handled in the determination of child support and alimony.
- When employee stock options convert to income and how that income should be measured is an area where there is little agreement. Should income only occur at time of exercise? Allowing the titled spouse to defer exercise may deprive the child of support.
- Whether employee stock options can be categorized as property for equitable distribution and utilized for child support varies across states. The classification is made more difficult when coverture ratios are used to allocate employee stock options as marital and separate property.

Note

1. *See* J. Blasi, D. Kruse & A. Berstein, In the Company of Owners: The Truth About Stock Options (And Why Every Employee Should Have Them) (Basic Books 2003).

When Are Employee Stock Options Marital Property?*

1

A. INTRODUCTION

Thirty-eight states have addressed the issue of employee stock options as marital or community property. All 38 states have held employee stock options to be property subject to distribution upon divorce, except when the facts of the individual case demonstrate that the property was acquired outside the period of marriage. However, whether all or some of granted but unvested employee stock options at the date of separation/date of complaint represent marital property is still an open issue in most jurisdictions. Not surprisingly, the extent to which granted but unvested options represent marital property is very much dependent upon the facts and circumstances of a particular matter.

B. ARE EMPLOYEE STOCK OPTIONS PROPERTY?

Employee stock options have attributes that often make it unclear whether they are assets or income, and if they are assets, whether they should be considered marital assets. Employee stock options typically vest over time, resulting in ownership rights that may not transfer until after the date

---

*   The authors would like to thank Rachel Branson, Jennifer Pao, and Joleen Okun, summer clerks at Schnader Harrison Segal & Lewis LLP, for their research assistance in the preparation of this chapter.

of separation/date of complaint. Furthermore, employee stock options generally are awarded "**at-the-money**," thus having no **intrinsic value** at the time of the award. Finally, employee stock options typically are nontransferable. Typically, at the time of the award or grant, employee stock options likely will have no intrinsic value, will be forfeited if employment ends, and cannot be transferred. That is, they have no fair market value. Whether a financial instrument without a fair market value should be considered property subject to equitable distribution was a subject of great debate in the 38 states that have ruled on this issue. The prevailing view is that employee stock options represent a contingent asset that should be considered an asset for equitable distribution in the same manner as pension assets.

In *Callahan v. Callahan,*[1] for example, the plaintiff-wife sought distribution of her husband's stock options that he acquired during the marriage. In challenging the distribution, the husband argued that the options did not constitute "property" subject to equitable distribution. He characterized stock options as a right to acquire an asset in the future. Additionally, he pointed out that stock options are limited because they are not transferable and terminate upon departure from the company. The court responded by asking the husband whether he could deny that "stock options represent property which, although not cash in hand, is not subject to a contingency, has a reasonably discernible value and awaits the owner to take actual possession?"[2] The court proceeded to compare stock options to pensions:

> [P]ensions . . . and the stock options here considered, represent types of property which are similar in a number of respects. Both constitute a form of compensation earned by the spouse during the marriage. Both are tied to respective plans which place some restriction on the enjoyment of the asset. For example, a pension may be deferred until retirement or termination of employment; the stock options here are withdrawn if the defendant terminates his employment with the corporation. The value of a pension at any particular time is generally calculable from the terms of the plan. Likewise, the option has a reasonably discernible value from the price of the stock.[3]

The husband went on to argue, however, that stock options are distinguishable from other forms of property subject to equitable distribution because money is required to exercise the option. The court determined that the expenditure required was not a crucial factor because the stock could be pledged against its cost. Therefore, after comparing stock options to pensions, the court found that stock options are also subject to equitable distribution.

The court's position in *Callahan* regarding the distribution of stock options was referenced by the New Jersey Supreme Court in *Kruger v. Kruger,*[4] which adjudicated the issue of the equitable distribution of military retirement pay. In finding future military retirement pay subject to distribution, the court stated:

> The *right* to receive monies in the future is unquestionably such an economic resource . . . No one would quarrel with the proposition that the recipient of a life estate created by a testamentary or inter vivos trust owned a valuable asset, which would be subject to equitable distribution. So, too, if one purchased or acquired an insurance annuity that paid a weekly sum certain to the beneficiary for life, the right to collect those funds would also be considered property subject to distribution. There are many different types of employee benefits, which employees or former employees receive, which everyone would readily admit are assets that have been acquired during employment. Deferred compensation, stock options, profit-sharing and pensions are typical examples.[5]

For example, in *Green v. Green,*[6] the Maryland Court of Special Appeals, in reversing the trial court's finding that a husband's irrevocable and nontransferable stock options acquired during the marriage, but unexercised before termination of the marriage, were not marital property, began its analysis by addressing whether stock options can be considered "property." The court compared restricted stock option plans to pension plans:

> As with pension plans, restricted stock option plans like those we consider here are a form of employee compensation, providing to the employee the right to accept within a prescribed time period and under certain conditions the corporate employer's irrevocable offer to sell its stock at the price quoted. If the employer attempts to withdraw that offer, "the employee

has a choice in action" in contract against the employer. We therefore conclude that stock option plans, like other benefits in an employee's compensation package constitute "property" as used in the definition of marital property.[7]

After establishing that stock options are property, the *Green* court decided that the options were marital property because they were acquired during the marriage. The *Green* and *Callahan* decisions are typical in that they treat unvested employee stock options as property. However, as discussed below, there is still wide divergence across states as to whether unvested employee stock options represent marital property.

C. ARE UNVESTED STOCK OPTIONS MARITAL PROPERTY?

Most states agree that employee stock options that vest during a marriage are marital property. However, many states have divergent views as to whether unvested stock options should be characterized as marital property. After a state has determined that stock options are an asset, the next step is to determine whether the options are part of the marital or community estate, or whether they are the separate property of the employee to whom the options were granted. Whether a stock option is classified as marital or nonmarital property varies by jurisdiction.

In Tennessee, for example, the status of stock options as marital property is codified: "Marital property includes . . . vested and unvested stock option rights . . . relating to employment that accrued during the period of the marriage."[8]

In general, whether the options are granted for services rendered or for future service is a key determinant of when the option has been earned. To the extent the employee stock option has been earned during the marriage, the option typically is considered marital property. Most cases are consistent in that they adhere to the concept that the benefits of employee stock options should be linked to when the benefits are earned, not when they are received. Relevant factors to determine whether employee stock options are granted for services rendered or for future services include:

- Whether the employee's current salary would be different if options were not granted. If so, this may indicate at least some component of the option grant is for services provided before date of grant.
- Whether the option award represents an infrequent bonus for superior performance. If so, this may indicate at least some component of the option grant is for services provided before date of grant.
- Whether the language of the stock option plan or stock option award letter states why options have been granted.

For example, in *Demo v. Demo,*[9] the husband was granted options to purchase 500 shares of stock with 125 shares vesting each year. The options were granted one year after the date of marriage. At the time of separation, the options had not yet been exercised. The option plan stated its purpose was "to provide special recognition and potential long-term value to key employees who demonstrate sustained high performance."[10] On appeal, the Ohio Appellate Court stated, "In this case, although the stock option was awarded to the appellee shortly after his marriage to appellant, the award was based upon job performance prior to the marriage. Therefore, appellee did not earn back the stock option during the marriage."[11]

In New Jersey, the cut-off date for identification of assets subject to equitable distribution is the date the divorce complaint is filed.[12] Nevertheless, the New Jersey Supreme Court considered stock options granted after the filing of the divorce complaint to be marital property: In *Pascale v. Pascale,*[13] the wife received options for 5,800 shares of her employer's stock 10 days after filing her divorce complaint. The wife argued that 1,800 shares were issued in recognition of past performance and the remaining shares reflected a job promotion that would impose additional future responsibilities. The wife further argued that the other 4,000 shares were nonmarital because they were not the fruits of her marital efforts. The court held that all of the shares were marital property because they all resulted from "efforts expended during the marriage."[14] Even though the options were granted shortly after the filing of the divorce complaint, the court included them in the marital estate to deter manipulation in timing the granting of options to a date after the complaint is filed. Regarding the wife's promotion and added responsibilities, arguably she would not have received the promotion but for certain contributions to the marriage by her husband. The court noted, "Like a spouse who cooks and cleans while one spouse rises to the top of a company, [husband] in his role as husband and father contributed in some way to the wife's successes, which increased her worth for that promotion."[15]

In *Chen v. Chen,*[16] the Wisconsin Court of Appeals held that options granted during the marriage that did not vest at the time of divorce were still considered marital property. "Although certain stock options are not exercisable until after the time of the divorce, they are nonetheless an economic resource acquired during the marriage. . . . The mere fact the interest in the asset is contingent does not mean that it may be ignored . . . [the husband] has failed to show what, if any, portion of the options' value is attributable to future efforts."[17]

The Wisconsin Court of Appeals stated in *Maritato v. Maritato*[18] that "the formula for [the] division [of options] derives from the facts of the individual case."[19] In that case, the court affirmed the trial court's marital property classification of the wife's stock options. The wife's stock options that had a market price greater than the exercise price were considered marital property because the options vested by the time the trial court wrote its decision. However, the wife's unvested options were not marital property. Even though the unvested stock options represented an economic resource under *Chen*, the options had been awarded only two months before the commencement of divorce, and the parties offered no evidence as to the present value of the options.[20]

Demo, Pascale, and *Chen* make strong statements as to whether unvested stock options representing marital property depend upon whether the options were earned during marriage. Most courts have made the connection between services provided by the employee-spouse and whether unvested stock options are marital property.

Some courts have used the date of vesting to represent when an option becomes marital property. For example, Indiana ruled in *Hann v. Hann*[21] that, because the titled spouse could not exercise the options until after the date of complaint, they were not marital property given that marital property consists only of property to which a party has title at the date of complaint.

The Illinois Court of Appeals also has held that unexercised stock options are not property until they are exercised.[22] This is an interesting conclusion in that only the titled spouse has the right to exercise

an employee stock option. Because employee stock options normally
have a life of 10 years, this may put a nontitled spouse at a distinct
financial disadvantage in wanting to exercise but not being able to
because the employee stock option is not property until exercise takes
place. In *In re Marriage of Linda L. Moody,*[23] the husband appealed
the lower court's decision to count his unexercised stock options as
marital property. He argued that the trial court's valuation was erroneous because the options had no value until they were exercised. The
trial court found the options subject to distribution because they were
acquired during the time of the marriage. In order to value the options
for division, the trial court improperly valued the options by taking
notice of the market price at which the stock traded the day before the
hearing and multiplying it by the number of shares. The Illinois Court
of Appeals agreed with husband and reversed the trial court's decision, finding that the trial court's use of the market price of the stock
the day before the hearing erroneous and that options do not have a
value until the time they are exercised. The court reasoned that:

> First, under the terms of the option agreements, the stock op-
> tions are nontransferable. . . . Respondent, therefore, would
> have to exercise the options in order to realize any profit. If
> they expire without ever being exercised, they have no value
> whatsoever. Second, on the date of the hearing, only 1,600,
> rather than 3,000, shares were exercisable under the restric-
> tions expressed in the agreements. Third, respondent presented
> evidence that his deteriorating health and lack of liquid capital
> make it impossible for him to exercise the options without
> obtaining a loan. Respondent would be required to raise a to-
> tal of $33,864 in order to exercise his rights under the agree-
> ments as of June 6, 1982. Finally, the margin requirements
> imposed by law restrict respondent from borrowing more than
> 50% of the full purchase price. Even if respondent were able
> to obtain a loan for that amount, he would have to raise almost
> $17,000 from his own sources. Given the above scenario, it is
> possible, if not probable, that respondent might never be able
> to exercise the options prior to the expiration dates of the pur-
> chase agreements.[24]

Interestingly, on remand, the court directed the lower court to retain jurisdiction over the stock options until exercised or expired, and

required the trial court to distribute the options if any future profit was realized by the husband. Illinois courts continue to hold that stock options are marital property only after they are exercised.[25]

In *Batra v. Batra*,[26] the husband received the right to purchase stock options before marriage, and the options were scheduled to expire two years after the parties' divorce. The wife argued that the time rule approved by a California court in the seminal case *In re Marriage of Hug*[27] should apply because she was entitled to a share of every portion of the original grant. However, the *Batra* court rejected the *Hug* time rule because, under that approach, the community would receive an interest in every portion of the remaining unvested options, even if the options vest several years after the divorce. The court in *Batra* asserted that employee stock options represent marital property only when they vest during a marriage.

> We recognize that stock options may be intended as a reward for past work or as an incentive for future service or any combination thereof. An award of yet to be vested stock options, such as those at issue here, which requires the employee spouse to continue as an employee throughout the vesting period, can easily be characterized as incentive options. Thus it makes little sense to invite the trial court to divine the intent behind the options. For these reasons, we adopt a single time-rule to be applied to the characterization of such options. . . . The communities interest is a fraction; the number of days of the marriage during the year of vesting of the flight of the stock option in question over the number of days in a year. The communities' interest in vesting flights of stock options is limited to those vesting in whole or in part during the years of marriage, eliminating whole years of vesting outside of the marriage and thereby hastening separation of the parties interests consistent with Idaho law.[28]

The *Batra* court favored this approach because it is an easy-to-apply, bright-line rule. In *Batra*, the marriage was prearranged and short-term. The wife came to this country, had a child, and then sought a divorce. The court's decision may have been influenced by these particular facts.

The significance of timing is also evident in *Clance v. Clance*.[29] In that case, the husband received a grant of stock options the day after the divorce was finalized. The wife argued on appeal that the stock options were marital property because all the effort leading up to the acquisition of the options occurred during the marriage. The husband argued that Missouri law considers marital property to be property that at least one party to the divorce has some enforceable right at the time of dissolution.[30] The Missouri Court of Appeals adopted this reasoning and held that the options received the day after the divorce for past services are not marital property.

A North Carolina court held that stock options that were granted but not exercisable on the date of separation were not marital property.[31] The court stated:

> [The rule] recognizes the purpose of stock options granted employees which are designed so that they vest and become exercisable over a period of time; such options represent both compensation for the employee's past services and incentives for the employee to continue in the employment in the future. Those options which have already vested are clearly rewards for past service rendered during the marriage, and therefore are marital property; options not yet vested are in essence, an expectation of a future right contingent upon continued service and should be considered separate property.[32]

To find the balance between unvested options as either all marital or all separate property, many courts have moved to a time-rule to allocate unvested options into marital and separate property based upon the facts and circumstances of a particular situation. It is often the situation that employee stock options are best characterized as being earned both before and after the date of separation as well as before and during the marriage.

D. TIME RULES USED TO DETERMINE WHAT PORTION OF STOCK OPTIONS ARE MARITAL PROPERTY

In *In re Marriage of Miller*,[33] the Colorado Supreme Court held that the marital portion of a stock option is determined based on which portion of those shares represents compensation for future services and which portion represents compensation for prior services.[34] The court held that options issued for past services may be fully marital upon issuance, unless a portion of the options are attributable to pre-marriage service. Conversely, employee stock options granted in consideration for future services are not marital property until the employee has performed those future services. The court remanded the case to the trial court to determine what portion of the options were granted for past services and what portion were granted for future services, so that the marital portion could be divided accurately between the parties.

The California Court of Appeals in *In re Marriage of Hug*[35] utilized what is known as a "time rule." The term "time rule" was clarified in the context of a pension in another case as a "formula for determining the community interest in pension benefits according to the ratio of the length of employment between the date of the marriage (or date of commencement of employment, if later) and the date of separation to the total length of employment."[36] In *Hug*, the court justified its use of the time rule in a stock options case as a means to "fairly allocate the stock options between compensation for services prior to and after the date of separation."[37]

Time rules to allocate the portion of employee stock options that are marital generally are based upon the ratio shown below:

$$\frac{\text{Date on which service began} - \text{Date on which marital efforts end}}{\text{Date on which service began} - \text{Date on which the option vests}}$$

The determination of the appropriate service period is highly fact specific and should be determined based upon a careful review of:

- The titled spouse's employment history;
- History of stock option awards;
- Review of stock option plan documents; and
- Review of employee stock option award letters.

The language in the plan documents and stock option award letters often provide insight into whether the employee stock option award is for past or future service. Shown below are excerpts from various employee stock plans. The first excerpt indicates that the option award is for past service along with a future work requirement.

This Plan for Professional and Other Highly Compensated Employees/Key Employees is designed to provide participants, as compensation in respect of past services rendered,

with a continuing long-term investment in the common stock of _____, the realization of which will be deferred to a future date.

This second excerpt clearly states the restricted stock award is for future service.

If your bonus is valued at $20,000 or more, the bonus you receive will have both a cash component, which represents an award for past performance, and a restricted stock component under the award, which represents an incentive for you to remain with the company.

This third plan excerpt is very general, and would seem to imply the employee option award is geared to reward employees for both past and future service.

The purpose of the Plan is to enable _____ and its subsidiaries to attract, retain and motivate officers and certain other employees, to compensate them for their contributions to the growth and profits of the Company.

When the employee stock option is granted for future service, the numerator of the above coveture fraction would begin with the date of the option grant. If, however, the option is granted for past service, the beginning date can be the date of employment, the date of marriage, or some other date that best captures when the option began to be earned.

In *Hug*,[38] the husband acquired three sets of options that did not vest and were not exercisable until after the date of separation. The court considered several factors to determine when the employee stock options were earned. The court considered all of the options granted to the husband before the separation to be both a reward for past services and incentive for future performance. The characterization of the options as both a reward and incentive was based on the court's understanding of the standard corporate purpose of stock options, which is to attract and retain executives and other key employees for the purpose of providing an incentive to stimulate increased effort.[39]

To value the husband's unvested stock options, the court used the following time rule formula to reflect the community component of the options that could not be exercised until after separation:

Number of months (or years) between commencement of
spouse's employment and date of parties' separation

Number of months (or years) between commencement
of spouse's employment
and date the options could be exercised (vested)

The numerator in the above formula represented the number of months/years the husband in the case worked at his company and was married to his wife. The denominator represented the number of months/years from the first day of employment to the time when an option could be first exercised. Then, the fraction is multiplied by the number of shares that could be purchased on the date the option was first exercisable; the remaining shares were deemed separate property of the employee-spouse.[40]

On appeal, the husband agreed that the property should be apportioned using a time rule, but argued that the trial court used the wrong rule. The proper time rule, according to the husband, would use the date the options were granted, not the date employment was commenced, because the options were not granted as an incentive for employment. Using the date of employment, the trial court implicitly contributed two more years of service the husband expended before receiving the options to the determination of the extent of the community property.[41]

In assessing the husband's argument on appeal, the court went into a detailed attempt to recategorize the purpose of stock options. These purposes included: (1) an alternative to fixed salaries; (2) attraction and retention of executives; and (3) additional compensation for past employment. In affirming the lower court's decision, the court found that the husband's argument relied too heavily on a single feature of the stock option agreement: The options having been granted for future services. In addition, the court found that the two-year period of service used in the lower court's calculation contributed to the granting of the stock options in question.[42] Thus, using the beginning of the option earning period as the latter of one's date of marriage or date of employment is now commonly called the *Hug* time rule.

In a later California decision, *In re Marriage of Nelson*,[43] the Court of Appeals modified the *Hug* time rule by beginning the period during which the options are earned on the date of option grant. In, *Nelson*, the husband's employer granted him three categories of options. The first group of options was granted and exercisable before the parties separated. These were held to be entirely community property. The second group was granted before separation, but not exercisable until after separation. These were characterized as partly community and partly separate property because they were granted for services rendered and services to be rendered. The third group was granted after separation. These were considered entirely separate property. However, the lower court modified the *Hug* time rule because it concluded that these options were granted exclusively to reward future service, whereas the stock options in *Hug* appeared to have been granted for multiple reasons, such as to attract employees, provide incentive for future services, and reward past employment. The *Nelson* court adopted the following modified *Hug* rule.

$$\frac{\text{Time between the signing or granting of the option agreement and date of separation}}{\substack{\text{Time from the signing or granting of the option} \\ \text{agreement and the day on whicheach} \\ \text{portion of the option became fully vested}}}$$

[handwritten margin note: grant date vs exer. date]

The court justified its decision by quoting the *Hug* court, stating "[no] single rule or formula is applicable to every dissolution case involving employee stock options . . . [The] trial court should exercise discretion to fashion an equitable allocation of separate and community interests in employee stock options exercisable by the employee-spouse after the date of separation of the parties."[44] On appeal, the wife unsuccessfully argued for the use of the original *Hug* time rule. The appellate court affirmed both the lower court's use of the modified time rule and the logic behind using the date the options were granted rather than the date of employment, as in *Hug*.[45]

The *Nelson* time rule produces quite a different outcome than the *Hug* time rule. In *Hug*, the husband had been granted 3,100 options to purchase his company's stock by the time he and his wife separated. The lower court determined that 1,835 option shares were subject to the time rule. Using its time rule, the *Nelson* Court categorized 1,299.37 of the 1,835 stock options as community property, and 535.63 as the husband's separate property. The wife received 50% of 70.8% of the options in question. As a community property state, all community assets are divided 50/50 upon divorce. If the *Nelson* time rule were applied to the facts in *Hug*, the wife would have received 50% of approximately 45% of the options in question. Thus, the time period the husband sought to remove from the *Hug* time rule proved to be very significant in *Nelson*.

Each state has its own guidelines as to the cut-off date to define or determine the marital or community estate. These guidelines must be incorporated in the time rule calculation. In *Salstrom v. Salstrom*,[46] for example, the husband received a series of three stock option packages. The first was exercisable during the marriage, but the latter two series were not exercisable until several years after the trial. Because the husband acquired a portion of these assets after entry of the divorce decree, the court determined that the options had marital and nonmarital components. In its decision, the lower court retained jurisdiction over the options until the time of vesting. The Minnesota Court of Appeals reversed, holding the better approach to be one that apportions the benefits using the *Nelson* time rule. The *Nelson* rule was modified to reflect Minnesota's cut-off date, which defines marital property as property acquired until the date of dissolution, unlike California where property is considered community property until the date the parties separate. Accordingly, in *Salstrom*, the Minnesota court used the following time rule:

$$\frac{\text{Total number of days between the signing or granting of the option agreement and the date of dissolution}}{\begin{array}{c}\text{Total number of days from the signing or granting of the option} \\ \text{agreement and the day on which each portion of the option} \\ \text{became fully vested and no longer subject to divestment}\end{array}}$$

The Court of Appeals of New York adopted and expanded upon *Miller*[47] in *DeJesus v. DeJesus*.[48]

> . . . the Miller court thus held that the marital portion of stock plans is a function of four separate calculations: (1) the relative shares traceable to past and future services must be determined; (2) any portions of the stock plans which are intended as compensation for past services are deemed marital property to the extent that the marriage coincides with the period of the

titled spouse's employment, up until the time of the grant; (3)
of that portion intended as incentive for future services, the
marital portion is determined by a time rule like that employed
by the California Court of Appeals in *In re Marriage of Nelson*,
177 Cal.App.3d 150, 222 Cal. Rptr. 790, supra, and (4) all
portions found to be marital property may be divided between
the spouses.[49]

As in *Miller*, the *DeJesus* court remanded the case for more testimony on whether the options were granted for past or future services. To make this determination, relevant factors included "whether the stock plans are offered as a bonus or as an alternative to fixed salary, whether the value or quantity of the employee's shares is tied to future performance and whether the plan is being used to attract key personnel from other companies."[50] Potential witnesses included the employee-spouse, human resources or benefits personnel from the employer, or a stock plan expert. To divide the options granted for past and future services, the court utilized two time rules, one for options granted for past services and one for future services. To factor out option value relating to the period before the marriage, the court employed the following time rule:

$$\frac{\text{Time from the beginning of employment or Date of marriage (whichever is later) until date of grant}}{\text{Time from the beginning of employment until the date of grant}}$$

For example, assume the following fact pattern for the grant of 12,000 employee options:

Date of Employment:	January 1, 1990
Date of Marriage:	January 1, 1992
Date of Option Grant:	January 1, 1996
Date of Separation:	January 1, 1998
Date of Vesting:	December 31, 2001

Using this fact pattern and the aforementioned time rule, two-thirds of the employee stock options (8,000 options) would be classified as marital property and one-third of the options (4,000 options) would be classified as separate property.

$$\frac{\text{January 1, 1992} - \text{January 1, 1996}}{\text{January 1, 1990} - \text{January 1, 1996}} = \frac{4}{6}$$

The same logic would exclude another segment of the options as being earned after separation using the following time rule:

$$\frac{\text{Time from the date of grant until date of separation}}{\text{Time from the date of grant until the date of vesting}}$$

$$\frac{\text{January 1, 1996} - \text{January 1, 1998}}{\text{January 1, 1996} - \text{January 1, 2001}} = \frac{2}{5}$$

Here, only 40% (3,200) of the remaining 8,000 marital options would be considered marital. Taken together, only 26.7% of the options (3,200 / 12,000) granted during marriage would be considered marital property under the premise that options are earned beginning on the date of employment and ending on the date of vesting.

When assessing the marital component of granted but unvested employee stock options, many jurisdictions now utilize a time rule where the date of grant sets the period for which service begins. This is based upon the premise that the grant is entirely for future service and that the employee-spouse's efforts and outcomes during the prior year before the grant played no role in the number of options granted. In *Robertson v. Robertson,*[51] the court indicated that, to the extent skills acquired during a marriage are utilized as a major factor in the assessment when options are earned, a supportive spouse is permitted to claim assets earned by the other spouse during their entire work life. Texas has recently codified its view on when service begins in determining the proportion of unvested stock options that are marital. **Coverture ratios** must now be based upon service beginning on the date of grant.[52] The impact of using different dates for when options are earned is demonstrated with the following example. Assume an employee-spouse who separated from the nonemployee-spouse on December 31, 2004, has been awarded options that vest after four years as set forth in Table 1-1.

Table 1-1
Grant and Vesting Schedule

Separates 12/31/2004

Grant ID#	Grant Date	# of Options Granted	Vesting Date	Date of Expiration
2002-78	2-Jan-03	10,000	31-Dec-2007	31-Dec-2012
2003-78	5-Jan-04	11,000	31-Dec-2008	31-Dec-2013
2004-78	2-Feb-05	10,500	31-Dec-2009	31-Dec-2014

Utilizing a coverture ratio for these three grants based upon a date of separation of December 31, 2004, results in 6,178 of the options classified as marital. See Table 1-2.

Table 1-2
Coverture Ratios

Grant ID#	Date of Grant - Date of Separation / Date of Grant - Date of Vesting	
	Coverture Fraction	Marital Component
1. 2002-78	$\dfrac{729 \text{ days}}{1{,}824 \text{ days}}$	
	40% marital	4,000 marital options
2. 2003-78	$\dfrac{361 \text{ days}}{1{,}822 \text{ days}}$	
	19.8% marital	2,178 marital options
		6,178 TOTAL

None of the options granted in February 2005 would be categorized as marital because they were granted after the date of separation However, if, based upon interviews with the employee-spouse, a review of the stock option plan document, and a discussion with members of the company's Human Resources department, it is clear that, although granted options are primarily for future service, the work effort during a year does play a role in the number of employee stock options granted to an individual employee, then one might want to begin the coverture ratio at June 30th of the year in which the grant

was earned. That way, 8,519 options would be considered marital by
asserting that the options were granted for service provided during the
year as well as for expected future contributions. See Table 1-3 for the
calculation.

Table 1-3
Coverture Ratios Using Date Service Begins

Date Service Begins (June 30th) – Date of Separation		
Date Service Begins (June 30th) – Date of Vesting		
Grant ID#	**Coverture Fraction**	**Marital Component**
1. 2002-78	$\dfrac{915 \text{ days}}{2010 \text{ days}}$	
	45.50% marital	4,550 marital options
2. 2003-78	$\dfrac{550 \text{ days}}{2,011 \text{ days}}$	
	27.3% marital	3,003 marital options
3. 2004-78	$\dfrac{184 \text{ days}}{2010 \text{ days}}$	
	9.2% marital	966 marital options
		8,519 TOTAL

The resulting 2,341 increase in marital options from 6,178 to 8,519
flows from a careful examination of the facts and circumstances, resulting in a better understanding of when the unvested employee stock
options are actually earned.

Furthermore, assume that the nonemployee-spouse helped finance
the employee-spouse's education during the early years of the marriage. A reasonable argument could be made that the options were
earned during the entire marriage even in a jurisdiction where the date
of the option grant normally is utilized for when service begins.

E. SUMMARY AND CONCLUSIONS

The decisions from the various states surveyed in this chapter provide
guidance to judges and attorneys dealing with stock options in di-

vorce cases. Although it seems clear that employee stock options represent property, states have taken highly divergent positions on whether options represent marital property. Time rules are often applied to allocate the portion of unvested employee stock options that should be considered marital. Although the *Hug* time rule has served as the starting point for most state courts, many courts have modified the original rule. The *Batra* court sought to create a bright-line rule, but even that court has yet to apply that rule to another case where the options vest after the parties separate.

Whether unvested employee stock options should be considered marital property most often is driven by the facts and circumstances surrounding each situation. For example, if it can be shown that the employee-spouse gave up cash compensation to receive stock options, there is a compelling case that they were granted at least in part for past service. An examination of salary history and firm compensation policy is a critical part of discovery. A review of stock option plan documents and award letters can provide insight into whether option grants represent a golden handcuff or a bonus for service provided.

Notes

1. 361 A.2d 561 (N.J. 1976).
2. *Id.* at 562.
3. *Id.* at 562–63.
4. 375 A.2d 659 (N.J. 1977).
5. *Id.* at 662 (emphasis added).
6. 494 A.2d 721 (Md. Ct. Spec. App. 1985).
7. *Id.* at 728.
8. TENN. CODE. ANN. § 36-4-121(b)(1)(B) (2005). *See also* Kyle v. Kyle, 2005 Tenn. App. LEXIS 87, at **27–28 (Tenn. Ct. App. Feb. 10, 2005) (Court applied § 36-4-121(b)(1)(B) to husband's vested stock options earned in the course of his employment).
9. 655 N.E.2d 791 (Ohio Ct. App. 1995).
10. *Id.* at 792.
11. *Id.*
12. *See* N.J. FAM. CODE § 9-4 (West 2004).
13. 140 N.J. 583, 660 A.2d 485 (N.J. 1995).
14. *Id.* at 609, 660 A.2d at 499.
15. *Id.* at 611, 660 A.2d at 499.
16. 416 N.W.2d 661 (Wis. Ct. App. 1987).
17. *Id.* at 662–63.
18. 685 N.W.2d 379 (Wis. Ct. App. 2004).
19. *Id.* at 387 (quoting *Chen*, 416 N.W.2d at 664).

20.   *Id.* at 386–387, 387 n.7.

21.   655 N.E.2d 566 (Ind. Ct. App. 1995).

22.   *See In re* Marriage of Linda L. Moody, 457 N.E.2d 1023 (Ill. App. Ct. 1983); *In re* Marriage of Frederick, 578 N.E.2d 612 (Ill. App. Ct. 1991); *In re* Marriage of Ackerley, 775 N.E.2d 1045 (Ill. App. Ct. 2002).

23.   457 N.E.2d at 1023.

24.   *Id.* at 1024.

25.   *See supra* note 22.

26.   17 P.3d 889 (Idaho Ct. App. 2001).

27.   201 Cal. Rptr. 676 (1984).

28.   *Batra,* 17 P.3d at 893.

29.   127 S.W.3d 716 (Mo. Ct. App. 2004).

30.   *See* MO. REV. STAT. § 452.330 (2004).

31.   Hall v. Hall, 363 S.E.2d 189 (N.C. 1987).

32.   *Id.* at 196.

33.   915 P.2d 1314 (Colo. 1996).

34.   *Id.* at 1316.

35.   201 Cal. Rptr. 676 (1984).

36.   *In re* Judd, 137 Cal. Rpt. 318 (Cal. App. 1977).

37.   *Hug,* 201 Cal. Rptr. at 679.

38.   *Id.* As noted above, some jurisdictions use the date of filing the divorce complaint or the date of the hearing as the relevant date in determining what is marital or community property.

39.   *Id.* at 681 (stating that stock options serve "the standard corporate purpose of "attracting and retaining the services of selected directors, executives and other key employees and for the purpose of providing an incentive to encourage and stimulate increased efforts by them.").

40.   *Id.* at 678.

41.   *Id.* at 684.

42.   *Id.*

43.   222 Cal. Rptr. 790 (Cal. Ct. App. 1986) (placing more emphasis on the period following each grant of options to the date of separation, than on the employee's entire tenure with the company up until the time of separation); *see also In re* Marriage of Harrison, 225 Cal. Rptr. 234 (Cal. Ct. App. 1986).

44.   *Nelson,* 222 Cal. Rptr. at 792–793.

45.   *Id.* at 790.

46.   404 N.W.2d 848 (Minn. Ct. App. 1987).

47.   See *supra* note 33 and accompanying text.

48.   687 N.E.2d 1319 (N.Y. 1997).

49.   *Id.* at 1323 (footnotes omitted).

50.   *Id.* at 1319.

51.   885 A.2d 470 (N.J. Super. Ct. App. Div. 2005).

52.   J. Loveless & W. Cole, *2005: The Year in Review: Family Law,* 69 TEX. B.J. 1, 36 (Jan. 2006).

Appendix 1-A
Nationwide Court Decisions on Stock Options as Marital Property

State	Case Name	Citation	Approach to Stock Options
Alabama	*Jennings v. Jennings*	490 So. 2d 10 (Ala. Civ. App. 1986)	Stock Options as Marital Property—No Time Rule
	Keff v. Keff	757 So. 2d 450 (Ala. Civ. App. 2000)	Stock Options as Marital Property—No Time Rule
Arizona	*In re the Marriage of William J. Brebaugh*	118 P.3d 43 (Ariz. Ct. App. 2005)	Stock Options as Marital Property—Time Rules Appropriate
	In re the Marriage of David M. Robinson and Angella S. Thiel	35 P.3d 89 (Ariz. Ct. App. 2001)	Stock Options as Marital Property—No Time Rule
Arkansas	*Richardson v. Richardson*	659 S.W.2d 510 (Ark. 1983)	Stock Options as Community Property—No Time Rule
California	*In re Marriage of Steinberger*	91 Cal. App. 4th 1449 (Cal. Ct. App. 2001)	*Hug* Time Rule
	In re Marriage of Vanderbeek	222 Cal. Rptr. 832 (Cal. Ct. App. 1986)	Stock Options as Community Property—No Time Rule
	In re Marriage of Hug	154 Cal. App. 3d 780 (Cal. Ct. App. 1984)	*Hug* Time Rule
	In re Marriage of Nelson	177 Cal. App. 3d 150 (Cal. Ct. App. 1986)	*Nelson* Time Rule
Colorado	*In re Marriage of Balanson*	25 P.3d 28 (Colo. 2001)	Stock Options as Marital Property—No Time Rule
	In re Marriage of Miller	915 P.2d 1314 (Colo. 1996)	Stock Options as Marital Property—Past vs. Future Services Test

State	Case Name	Citation	Approach to Stock Options
Connecticut	*Bornemann v. Bornemann*	752 A.2d 978 (Conn. 1998)	*Hug* Time Rule
	Wendt v. Wendt	757 A.2d 1225 (Conn. App. Ct. 2000)	*Nelson* Time Rule
Delaware	*In re Marriage of Fatora*	No. CN95-10406, 1998 Del. Fam. Ct. LEXIS 195, at *1 (Del. Fam. Ct. 1998)	Time Rule Using Date of Marriage to Date of Initial Exercisability
Florida	*Ruberg v. Ruberg*	858 So. 2d 1147 (Fla. Dist. Ct. App. 2003)	Stock Options as Marital Property—Options for Future Service.
	Griffing v. Griffing	772 So. 2d 979 (Fla. 5th D.C.A. 1999)	Stock Options as Marital Property—No Time Rule
	Langevin v. Langevin	698 So. 2d 601 (Fla. Dist. Ct. App. 1997)	Stock Options as Marital Property—No Time Rule
	Jensen v. Jensen	407 So. 2d 1104 (Fla. Dist. Ct. App. 1981)	Stock Options as Marital Property—No Time Rule
	Parry v. Parry	2004-2109 (Fla. Dist. Ct. App. 2005)	Stock Options as Marital Property—Time Rule Appropriate
Georgia	*Thomas v. Thomas*	377 S.E.2d 666 (Ga. 1989)	Stock Options as Marital Property—No Time Rule
Idaho	*Batra v. Batra*	17 P.3d 889 (Idaho Ct. App. 2001)	*Batra* Time Rule
Illinois	*In re Marriage of Ackerley*	775 N.E.2d 1045 (Ill. App. Ct. 2002)	Stock Options as Marital Property—No Time Rule

State	Case Name	Citation	Approach to Stock Options
Illinois	*In re Marriage of Linda L. Moody*	457 N.E.2d 1023 (Ill. App. Ct. 1983)	Stock Options as Marital Property—No Time Rule
Indiana	*Hann v. Hann*	655 N.E.2d 566 (Ind. Ct. App. 1995)	*Nelson* Time Rule
	Knotts v. Knotts	693 N.E.2d 962 (Ind. Ct. App. 1998)	Stock Options as Marital Property—No Time Rule
	Henry v. Henry	758 N.E.2d 991 (Ind. Ct. App. 2001)	Stock Options as Marital Property—No Time Rule
Iowa	*In re Marriage of Milton*	No. 00-0616, 2002 WL 1840858, at *1 (Iowa. App. Aug. 14, 2002)	Stock Options as Marital Property—No Time Rule
Louisiana	*Hansel v. Holyfield*	779 So. 2d 939 (La. Ct. App. 2000)	Stock Options as Community Property—No Time Rule
Maryland	*Otley v. Otley*	810 A.2d 1 (Md. Ct. App. 2002)	*Nelson* Time Rule
	Green v. Green	494 A.2d 721 (Md. Ct. Spec. App. 1985)	Stock Options as Marital Property—No Time Rule
Massachusetts	*Baccanti v. Morton*	752 N.E.2d 718 (Mass. 2001)	Time Rule Including the Pre-marital Time Period
Michigan	*Everett v. Everett*	489 N.W.2d 111 (Mich. Ct. App. 1992)	Stock Options as Marital Property—No Time Rule
Minnesota	*Hislop v. Hislop*	No. DC200572, 1998 Minn. App. LEXIS, 951, at *1 (Minn. Ct. App. Aug. 18, 1998)	*Nelson* Time Rule
	In re Marriage of Salstrom	404 N.W.2d 848 (Minn. Ct. App. 1987)	*Nelson* Time Rule

State	Case Name	Citation	Approach to Stock Options
Missouri	*Clance v. Clance*	127 S.W.3d 716 (Mo. Ct. App. 2004)	Stock Options as Marital Property—No Time Rule
	Warner v. Warner	46 S.W.3d 591 (Mo. Ct. App. 2001)	Stock Options as Marital Property—No Time Rule
	Smith v. Smith	682 S.W.2d 834 (Mo. 1984)	Stock Options as Marital Property—No Time Rule
Nebraska	*Davidson v. Davidson*	578 N.W.2d 848 (Neb. 1998)	*DeJesus* Time Rule and *Short* Time Rule
New Hampshire	*In re Valence*	798 A.2d 35 (N.H. 2002)	Case Remanded to Trial Court for Determination of Relevant Time Rule
New Jersey	*Robertson v. Robertson*	A 2282-03T2 (N.J. 2005)	Options granted for Future Service not Marital Property
	Pascale v. Pascale	660 A.2d 485 (N.J. 1995)	Stock Options as Marital Property—No Time Rule
	Callahan v. Callahan	361 A.2d 561 (N.J. Ch. 1976)	Stock Options as Marital Property—No Time Rule
New Mexico	*Garcia v. Mayer*	920 P.2d 522 (N.M. Ct. App. 1996)	*Hug* Time Rule
New York	*DeJesus v. DeJesus*	687 N.E.2d 1319 (N.Y. 1997)	*DeJesus* Time Rule
North Carolina	*Hall v. Hall*	363 S.E.2d 189 (N.C. Ct. App. 1987)	Stock Options as Marital Property—No Time Rule

State	Case Name	Citation	Approach to Stock Options
Ohio	*Berthelot v. Berthelot*	796 N.E.2d 541 (Ohio Ct. App. 2003)	Stock Options as Marital Property—No Time Rule
	Demo v. Demo	655 N.E.2d 791 (Ohio Ct. App. 1995)	Stock Options as Marital Property—No Time Rule
Oklahoma	*Ettinger v. Ettinger*	637 P.2d 63 (Okla. 1991)	Stock Options as Marital Property—No Time Rule
Oregon	*In re Marriage of Taraghi*	977 P.2d 453 (Or. Ct. App. 1999)	*Nelson* Time Rule
	In re Marriage of Powell	934 P.2d 612 (Or. Ct. App. 1997)	Time Rule
Pennsylvania	*MacAleer v. MacAleer*	725 A.2d 829 (Pa. Super. Ct. 1999)	Stock Options as Marital Property—No Time Rule
	Fisher v. Fisher	769 A.2d 1165 (Pa. 2001)	Stock Options as Marital Property—No Time Rule
South Carolina	*Bungener v. Bungener*	353 S.E.2d 147 (S.C. Ct. App. 1987)	Stock Options as Marital Property—No Time Rule
Tennessee	*Brandon v. Brandon*	1999 Tenn. App. LEXIS 271 *12–13 (Tenn. Ct. App. April 29, 1999)	Stock Options as Marital Property—No Time Rule
	Kyle v. Kyle	2005 Tenn. App. LEXIS 87, at **27–28 (Tenn. Ct. App. Feb. 10, 2005)	Stock Options as Marital Property—Case Remanded to Determine the Number of Options Acquired during Marriage.
Texas	*Boyd v. Boyd*	67 S.W.3d 398 (Tex. App. 2002)	Stock Options as Community Property—No Time Rule

State	Case Name	Citation	Approach to Stock Options
Texas	*Charriere v. Charriere*	7 S.W.3d 217 (Tex. App. 1999)	Stock Options as Community Property—No Time Rule
Utah	*Argyle v. Argyle*	688 P.2d 468 (Utah 1984)	Stock Options as Marital Property—No Time Rule
Virginia	*Ott v. Ott*	No. 0614-00-1, 2001 Va. App. LEXIS 10, at *1 (Va. Ct. App. Jan. 16, 2001)	Stock Options as Marital Property—No Time Rule
	Tatum v. Tatum	No. 0438-00-3, 2000 Va. App. LEXIS 789, at *1 (Va. Ct. App. Dec. 5, 2000)	Stock Options as Marital Property—No Time Rule
	Ranney v. Ranney	608 S.E.2d 485 (Va. Ct. App. 2005)	Stock Options as Marital Property—No Time Rule
Washington	*In re Marriage of Short*	890 P.2d 12 (Wash. 1995)	*Short* Time Rule
	In re Marriage of Stachofsky	951 P.2d 346 (Wash. Ct. App. 1998)	*Hug* Time Rule
	In re Marriage of Harrington	935 P.2d 1357 (Wash. Ct. App. 1997)	Stock Options as Marital Property—No Time Rule
West Virginia	*Kapfer v. Kapfer*	419 S.E.2d 464 (W. Va. 1992)	Stock Options as Marital Property—No Time Rule
Wisconsin	*In re Marriage of Chen*	416 N.W.2d 661 (Wis. Ct. App. 1987)	*Hug* Time Rule
	Metko v. Metko	630 N.W.2d 276 (Wis. Ct. App. 2001)	Stock Options as Marital Property—No Time Rule
	Maritato v. Maritato	685 N.W.2d 379 (Wis. Ct. App. 2004)	Stock Options Sometimes Marital Property

Appendix 1-B
Basic Information Request for Valuing Executive Stock Options

In order to determine when executive stock options have been earned as well as their value, the following information should be collected and reviewed:

____ Schedule of granted options between relevant dates which indicate:
- Date of each option grant
- Number of options granted at each date
- Exercise price of options granted at each date
- Expiration date for each set of options granted
- Date of vesting for each set of options granted
- Date and number of any options exercised

____ Company information to gain insight into why the firm awards executive stock options, how the firm values stock options, and what constitutes the employee's compensation package, including:
- All short-term or long-term employee incentive plans covering the titled spouse
- All employee stock option grant letters
- All employment agreements with titled spouse
- All company plans, handbooks, memoranda, etc. related to employee stock options granted
- Copies of the firm's 10K and 8K

____ Employee background information to develop a better understanding of how the executive stock options fit into the overall compensation package of the individual. This information can be important in determining the type of coverture ratio, which might be applied to determine the percentage of option value, classified as marital.
- Educational history
- Employment history
- Date of hire of each full-time job

- Name of employer
- Date of promotions
- Positions held
- Brief job description of each position
- Salary history indicating all forms of compensations

Employee Stock Option Valuation

2

A. INTRODUCTION

Traded stock options have value because they provide investors greater upside potential for gain with limited downside risk relative to purchasing shares of the underlying security outright. However, unless the underlying security experiences significant stock price movements up or down, the option investor will earn less of a return than the investor who purchases the security outright. Employee stock options are different from traded stock options in two material respects. First, employee stock options generally have an **expiration date** that is longer than traded stock options. All else being equal, this attribute increases the value of employee stock options relative to traded stock options. Second, employee stock options typically are not transferable. This lack of marketability reduces the value of employee stock options relative to traded stock options.

B. WHY STOCK OPTIONS HAVE VALUE

Stock options that provide the option holder the right as opposed to the obligation to purchase a certain quantity of the company's stock at a specified price (the exercise or strike price) over a specified period of time are classified as **call options.**[1] To a large extent, the flexibility afforded an option holder in the right to buy stock at a fixed price as opposed to the obligation to purchase provides

29

the basis for a stock option's value. To develop an understanding of option terminology and how this flexibility provides value, let us first look at Apple Computer, Inc. traded stock options.

Table 2-1
Apple Computer, Inc. Traded Stock Options

Apple Computer (AAPL) Share Price Jan. 6, 2006: $76.30					
	Exercise Price or Strike Price	Expiration Date	Cost or Market Value	Intrinsic Value	Time Value
1	$75.00	Feb. 17, 2006	$5.10	$1.30	$3.80
2	$75.00	Jan. 19, 2007	$15.10	$1.30	$13.80
3	$75.00	Jan. 18, 2008	$21.10	$1.30	$19.80
4	$85.00	Feb. 17, 2006	$1.50	$(8.70)	$10.20
5	$85.00	Jan. 19, 2007	$11.00	$(8.70)	$19.70
6	$85.00	Jan. 18, 2008	$19.00	$(8.70)	$27.70

On January 6, 2006, Apple Computer's share price closed at $76.30. For our purposes, we will examine Apple Computer traded call options with an exercise price of $75 and $85 as shown on Table 2-1, above. An option's exercise price (or strike price) represents the fixed purchase price at which an option holder can purchase stock through the expiration date. Thus, as illustrated on Table 2-1, option 2 allows an investor to purchase a share of Apple Computer for $75 through January 19, 2007.

The market value, or cost, of the option is the amount the investor must pay to acquire an option. An option's cost or market value is often referred to as the option's premium. Option 2 has a $15.10 market value.

The difference between a security's share price and the exercise price of an option on that security is defined as the option's **intrinsic value**. An option with a positive intrinsic value is called an **in-the-money stock option**. Options 1 through 3 are all in-the-money because the $75.00 exercise price is less than Apple Computer's share price of $76.30.

An **out-of-the-money stock option** occurs when the exercise price of the option is greater than the share price of the security. Options 4 through 6 are all out-of-the-money because the exercise price of $85 is greater than Apple's share price of $76.30. When an option's exercise price equals the underlying security's share price the option is categorized as an **at-the-money stock option.**

An option's **time value** is the difference between the market value of an option and its intrinsic value. As shown in Table 2-1, the time value of option 2 is $13.80. That is, investors paid $13.80 on January 6, 2006, beyond the option's intrinsic value ($1.30) for the ability to purchase a share of Apple stock for $75 through January 19, 2007.

It is worth noting that even out-of-the money options have value. Options 4 through 6 all had an exercise price of $85 while the Apple Computer shares were trading at $76.30. However, as shown in Table 2-1, all these options have value as indicated by their market values. The fundamental question is, why are investors willing to pay beyond what they would have to pay to purchase Apple shares outright?

Assume Investor A purchases Apple Computer shares outright for $76.30, and over the next year Apple Computer's stock price drops in value to $51.30 per share. The investor will suffer a loss of $25 per share. Assume Investor B purchased for $15.10 Apple Computer options that have an exercise price of $75 and expire February 2007. Because the price of Apple shares have fallen, Investor B will choose not to exercise the option. Investor B will lose the option cost of $15.10; the downside risk to the option holder is limited to the cost of the option. Investor A will suffer a greater loss of value. The downside risk for Investor A is much greater. Thus, one advantage of options is that option holders have less downside risk than do those who purchase shares outright.

Nevertheless, option holders have the potential for greater returns than those who purchase shares outright. Assume that Apple Computer shares increase in value to $100 per share over the next year.

Table 2-2
Impact of Share Price Increase

Investor A	
Purchase 100 shares of Apple Computer @ 76.30	(7,630.00)
Sell 100 shares one year later at $100 per share	10,000.00
Pre-tax Gain	**2,370.00**
Rate of Return	**31%**
Investor B	
Purchase 505.3 options @ $15.10 per option	(7,630.00)
Exercise options & purchases 505.3 shares @ $75 per share	(37,897.50)
Sell 505.3 shares @ $100 per share	50,530.00
Pre-tax Gain	**5,002.50**
Rate of Return	**66%**

As shown on Table 2-2, Investor A purchased 100 shares of Apple Computer stock outright and ended up with a $2,370 gain (31% rate of return). Investor B purchased the same dollar value of options but ended up with a $5,002.50 gain (66% rate of return). This is because options provide leverage to investors by allowing them to control shares of stock for less than the full cost of the share. In this example, Investor B controls a share of Apple Computer for the option cost of $15.10. This allows Investor B to purchase 505.3 options, whereas Investor A can only purchase 100 shares for the same $7,630 investment. This leverage provides the option holder the opportunity to earn high rates of return if the underlying security increases in price over the life of the option. This potential for greater return with downside risk protection is why options have value.

Option holders will not always do better than those who purchase shares outright. If the share price of Apple Computer only slightly increases or decreases, Investor A, who purchased the shares outright, will have done better than Investor B. As shown on Table 2-3, if Apple Computer shares moved in price from $76.30 to $83.30, Investor A will have realized a gain of $700.

Table 2-3
Impact of Share Price Decrease

Investor A	
Purchase 100 shares of Apple Computer @ 76.30	(7,630.00)
Sell 100 shares a year later at $83.30 per share	8,330.00
Pre-tax Gain	**700.00**
Rate of Return	**9%**
Investor B	
Purchase 505.3 options @ $15.10 per option	(7,630.00)
Exercise options & purchases 505.3 shares @ $75 per share	(37,897.50)
Sell 505.3 shares @ $83.30 per share	50,530.00
Pre-tax Gain	**(3,536.01)**
Rate of Return	**-45%**

Investor B will suffer a loss of $3,436.01 because the option cost $15.10, whereas the price of the stock only increased by $7.00 per share. The option holder will outperform the investor, who purchased shares outright, when the share price of the underlying security makes large moves up or down. As a result, option holders prefer securities whose returns are highly volatile.

The expected life of the option also impacts value. As shown on Table 2-1, Apple Computer options traded with the same exercise price have a greater value the further into the future the option's expiration date. Apple options, with an exercise price of $85 and an expiration date in five weeks (February 17, 2006), were trading at $1.50 while the same options that expire in two years (January 18, 2008) were trading at $19.00. Clearly, waiting two years to purchase Apple Computer shares at $85 per share (current price $76.30) has more value than waiting only a few weeks.

In summary, traded options have value because they provide investors greater opportunity to earn high rates of return with limited downside risk. This feature exists because options holders have the right but not obligation to acquire shares of stock at a fixed price. This right provides value to options, even those that are out-of-the money.

This reality is critical to family law attorneys when determining the net worth of an individual at any given point in time.

C. HOW OPTIONS ARE VALUED

How options are valued can best be understood by the use of decision trees.[2] Assume that a share of stock is currently trading at $30, and there is a 50% chance the stock will either increase to $36 or fall to $24 per share next year. If the stock price goes to $36 next year, the share price will increase to $43 per share or fall back to $30 per share in year two. If the share falls to $24 next year, in year two the share price may increase back to $30 per share or continue to fall in price to $19 per share. Potential share prices for the next two years are shown in Table 2-4.

Table 2-4
Expected Share Prices for the Next Two Years

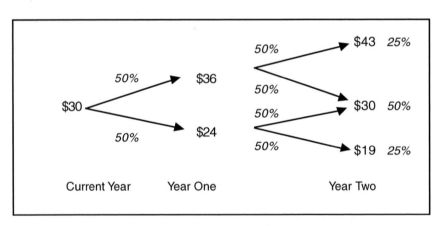

What will an investor pay for a two-year option with an exercise price of $30? Keep in mind that the option is at-the-money (a zero intrinsic value). As shown on Table 2-5, if the price of stock goes to $43 per share at the end of two years, the option holder will earn $13 after exercising the option. If the share price stays at $30 or falls to $19 at the end of year two, the options are worthless and will not be exercised.

As shown on Table 2-5, there is a 25% chance that the option holder will earn $13.00. Ignoring time value considerations for this example, the option will have a current value of $3.25 (25% of $13).

Table 2-5
Option Values Given Expected Outcomes

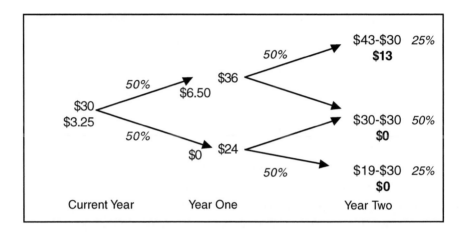

We see options that provide the ability to purchase shares at the current share price of $30 per share, a zero intrinsic value, will have value because there is a positive probability that the current share price will increase over time, generating an investment gain. If the share price falls, however, the option holder will not exercise and the loss is limited to the cost of the option.

Extension of the valuation logic from the simple decision tree discussed above to several periods along with other refinements was initially accomplished by Fisher Black and Myron Scholes. Myron Scholes won the 1997 Nobel Prize in economics for his research in option valuation.[3] The **Black-Scholes Option Pricing Model (BSOPM)** determines value by estimating five key variables. These variables are:

- The intrinsic value of the option;
- The volatility of the returns of the underlying stock;
- The **risk-free rate** of interest;
- The expected life of the option; and
- The **dividend yield** of the underlying stock.

Consider the option in our example that has an exercise price of $30 and underlying stock price of $30. If a second option existed with the same features and an exercise price of $25.00, the second option would have an intrinsic value of $5.00. The option certainly would have greater value than $3.25, given the intrinsic value of $5.00. We can see that the greater the intrinsic value of an option, the greater its value.

Increased volatility also positively impacts the option value. "**Volatility**" means the range of possible future share prices and the resulting potential gains and losses. In Table 2-4, share prices can range from $19 to $43 after two years. Unlike most assets, option values rise with increases in volatility. The reason is that downside volatility is not important to an option holder in that an option at or out of the money will not be exercised.

In fact, it does not matter if the future stock price falls to $19.00 or $5.00, the option will expire worthless. If in the future the share prices can rise to $60 instead of $43, however, the option value will rise as potential for gain increases. That means that upside volatility can create large positive payoffs. The asymmetric nature of the outcome means that volatility is a positive factor in option pricing. To accurately value an option, the expected volatility of returns must be estimated. Two approaches for measuring volatility are the historical method and the implicit method. Both of these methods are discussed in the next section of this chapter.

When interest rates rise, option prices will also have slightly higher values. This is because the capital outlay for an option is lower than the price of the actual stock. The remaining money can be invested to purchase additional options or other assets.

When we compare the expected life of an option, we note that the greater the life, the greater the option value. The longer an investor can wait for the underlying share price to increase, the more valuable the option because the exercise price of the option typically is fixed.

The dividend yield also impacts the option value. An option holder does not have claim on paid dividends. Dividends represent an opportunity cost to the option investor. The present value of forgone dividends lost to the option investor reduces option value.

The BSOPM integrates these factors into a valuation model. Although the mathematics of the model are complex, implementation is not. Like any other valuation model, when an analyst makes reasonable assumptions around the factors outlined above, the resulting estimate of option value will also be reasonable. With this in mind, we now move on to look at the valuation of employee stock options using the BSOPM.

D. DIFFERENCES BETWEEN TRADED AND EMPLOYEE STOCK OPTIONS—NONTRANSFERABILITY AND THE EXPECTED HOLDING PERIOD[4]

The discussion above was based upon tradable options. Employee stock options are not tradable. As a result, the value of an employee stock option at any point in time may not be realizable. For example, the Apple Computer option that has an exercise price of $85 that expires in 2008 (Table 2-1, Option 6) was trading at $19.00 on January 6, 2006. Assume, however, that an Apple Computer employee was granted Apple Computer options with the same characteristics as Option 6, except that it was not tradable. Is the employee stock option still worth $19.00? The option cannot be sold or transferred; therefore, on January 6, 2006, the employee holds an option with a negative intrinsic value and no fair market value. But the option clearly has a value to the employee. How the lack of marketability impacts the value to the employee is an important issue in the valuation of employee stock options. As discussed below, the lack of marketability of employee stock options enters the BSOPM through a reduction in the **expected holding period.**

Nalin Kulatilaka and Alan Marcus[5] provide theoretical support for the proposition that employee stock options on average will be exercised earlier than dictated by option models focusing on traded options. They concluded that, "early exercise will be more pronounced and the value of options will be lower when employees are more risk averse and when a larger fraction of total compensation is in the form of options."[6]

According to Kulatilaka and Marcus, the factors that determine whether the option is exercised early are:

1. An employee's level of risk aversion;
2. The proportion of overall wealth the options represent to an individual; and
3. The volatility of stock return for the underlying security.

Risk aversion deals with the trade-off between a certain return and a risky return. The classic example is as follows. Alternative 1 offers an individual an investment opportunity that will cost $1,000 and has a guaranteed return of $1,100 one year from now. Alternative 2 also requires an investment of $1,000 and will return either $800 or $1,400 one year from now. Thus, the expected return is also $1,100. Given that the expected returns are the same, all risk-averse individuals will choose Alternative 1 because Alternative 2 involves more risk yet provides the investor with the same expected return. An individual with very little risk aversion might accept Alternative 2 if the projected returns increased to $800 or $1,600 in one year because the expected return would then be $1,200. An investor who is very risk averse would probably not be willing to accept Alternative 2 unless the greatest possible return increased to at least $2,000.

Individuals who prefer low-risk, low-return investment portfolios generally are classified as more risk averse, whereas individuals with compensation packages that are more variable (e.g., compensation is commission based) would be viewed as less risk averse. Kulatilaka and Marcus demonstrate that the lower the level of risk aversion for an individual, the longer the time frame before they exercise their options.

S. Huddart[7] provides a theoretical model that indicates executive stock options will be exercised before expiration based upon the risk aversion of the executive. In his model, Huddart provides a simulation of when employee stock options might be exercised based upon what he calls the plausible assumptions regarding risk aversion and other underlying factors. In his article, the expected time to exercise varies between 4.8 years and 9.4 years, depending upon the individual's degree of risk aversion.[8]

Empirical research also provides insight into the expected holding period of employee stock options. Jennifer Carpenter[9] collected a sample of executive stock options issued by 40 firms between 1979 and 1994 and found that the average option was exercised in 5.83 years with the median time to exercise at just over six years. In addition, the stock price averaged 2.8 times the exercise price when the option was exercised. Carpenter concludes:

> Existing models of the optimal exercise policy for an executive who cannot sell or hedge his option demonstrate that with sufficiently high risk aversion and low wealth, the executive

who exercised the option almost as soon as he gets in the money making its value arbitrarily small. I show that such extreme behavior is not consistent with exercise patterns observed in the data. Executives hold options longer enough and deep enough into the money before exercising to capture a significant amount of their potential value.[10]

Huddart and Lang[11] examined the exercise behavior of over 50,000 employees who held long-term options at eight corporations. Their analysis indicated that early exercise is strongly associated with recent stock price movements, the ratio of market to strike price, time to maturity, volatility, and the employees' level within the company. Average time to exercise in their sample was 3.4 years, and the average ratio of stock price to exercise price was 2.2. However, the dividend yields of the companies in the sample are five percent, which would contribute to an earlier exercise. In addition, because employees in these firms came from all levels as opposed to just senior executives, we would expect the option holder to be less affluent, more risk averse, and therefore more likely to generate an early exercise. Their data was consistent with Carpenter's in her 1998 article, where options were held again for an average of 5.8 years.[12]

The accounting profession has also accepted the proposition that employee stock options on average will be exercised before their expiration. SFAS 123, promulgated in 1995 and restated in 2004, states:

> The value of a transferable option is based upon its maximum term because it rarely is economically advantageous to exercise, rather than sell, a transferable option before the end of its contractual term. Employee stock options differ from other options in that employees cannot sell their options—they can only exercise them. To reflect the effect of employees' inability to sell their vested options, this Statement *requires that the value of an employee stock option be based on its expected life rather than its maximum term.*[13]

We see the implementation of SFAS 123 in public company financial statements. Shown below is part of the employee stock option disclosure Johnson & Johnson made in their 2004 financial statements[14]:

The average fair value of options granted was $13.11 in 2004, $13.58 in 2003, and $15.49 in 2002. The fair value was estimated using the Black-Scholes option pricing model based on the weighted average assumptions of:

	2004	2003	2002
Risk-free rate	3.15%	3.09%	4.39%
Volatility	27.0%	28.0%	26.0%
Expected life	**5.0 yrs**	**5.0 yrs**	**5.0 yrs**
Dividend yield	1.76%	1.35%	1.33%

The following table summarizes stock options outstanding and exercisable at January 2, 2005:

(Shares in Thousands)	Outstanding			Exercisable	
Exercise Price Range	Options	Average Life(1)	Average Exercise Price	Options	Average Exercise Price
$ 3.85 - $ 22.95	11,336	**1.4**	$20.18	11,329	$20.18
$ 23.11 - $ 39.86	22,703	**3.1**	30.46	22,048	30.45
$ 40.08 - $ 50.08	34,952	**4.7**	46.00	34,615	45.98
$ 50.11 - $ 52.11	31,953	5.8	50.70	31,371	50.69
$ 52.20 - $ 53.89	39,403	8.1	52.22	173	52.48
$ 53.93 - $ 54.89	46,012	9.1	53.95	399	54.69
$ 55.01 - $ 65.10	42,645	7.1	57.34	553	59.20
	229,004	**6.4**	**$48.62**	**100,488**	**$ 41.26**

(1) Average contractual life remaining in years.

As indicated, Johnson & Johnson employee stock options were valued using the BSOPM. The average expected life for employee stock options granted for the past three years used in the valuation was five years. The distribution of outstanding options indicates that many unexercised options have been outstanding for 7 to 9.5 years. For example, 22,703 options with an average exercise price of $30.45 were issued on average seven years ago. This tells us that option valuation with the estimated average life of five years must be applied with caution because many option holders have been holding on to their options for a significantly longer time period.

The reduction in the holding period can have a large impact on the value of employee stock options as shown on Table 2-6. Traded Johnson

& Johnson options with an exercise price of $55 have an intrinsic value of $7.52 ($62.52 – $55.00), indicating these options are in-the-money. The market value of the option expiring in five weeks (Feb. 17, 2006) is only $.33 beyond its intrinsic value, whereas the option expiring in two years (Jan. 18, 2008) has a market value of $12.15 that is $4.63 beyond its intrinsic value.

Table 2-6
Johnson & Johnson Traded Stock Options

Johnson & Johnson
Share Price Jan. 6, 2006: $62.52

Exercise Price	Expiration Date	Intrinsic Value	Market Value	Premium of Market Value to Intrinsic Value
$55.00	Feb. 17, 2006	$7.52	$7.85	$3.80
$55.00	Jan. 18, 2008	$7.52	$12.15	$13.80
Impact of greater holding period			**$4.30**	**55% increase in value**
$65.00	Feb. 17, 2007	$(2.48)	$0.55	$3.03
$65.00	Jan. 18, 2008	$(2.48)	$6.15	$8.63
Impact of greater holding period			**$5.60**	**1,018% increase in value**

This make good economic sense in that waiting two years for Johnson and Johnson's share price to increase is worth more than waiting only five weeks. The longer holding period increased the value of the option by $4.30 ($4.63 – $.33).

The Johnson & Johnson stock options with an exercise price of $65.00 have a negative intrinsic value (–$2.48), indicating that they are out-of-the money. However, investors are paying $.55 to buy the option expiring in five weeks because there is some positive likelihood that Johnson & Johnson's share price will increase over this time period. However, investors are willing to pay $6.15 for the Johnson & Johnson stock option with the same exercise price, which expires in two years. Again, this makes good economic sense because the probability of Johnson & Johnson stock increasing in value over the next two years is greater than the probability of it increasing in value over the next five weeks. Thus, investors are willing to pay more for the option with a longer duration.

We also observe that the impact on option value from a change in the holding period is sensitive to the spread between the option's exercise price and the underlying securities share price. In the above example, the increase in the holding period by one year of the Johnson & Johnson option with a $55 exercise price increased the option value by 55%. For the out-of-the-money option, the increase in the holding period increased option value by over 1,000%. In general, the market value of options with an exercise price that is close to that of the underlying security price is quite sensitive to the life of the option.

Family law attorneys must pay close attention to holding period used to value employee stock options as part of a marital property settlement. Employee stock options often have a contractual life of 10 years. For the Johnson & Johnson options with an exercise price of $65, the value of one option would be approximately $12 using the BSOPM. This is in contrast to its current negative intrinsic value.

However, employee stock options, which cannot be traded, likely will be exercised before their expiration date. Both financial theory and empirical evidence, as discussed below, support this proposition. Thus, when valuing employee stock options, the expected life of the option should be the determining factor to avoid overstating the option's value by using the contractual term of the option. Using the expected life of an option in implementing the BSOPM—as is the practice of most public companies—addresses the lack of marketability inherent in employee stock options.

There are several resources available to form an estimate of the expected holding period used to value employee stock options. When employee stock options are granted on a regular basis, one can observe the exercise history of the titled spouse. Of course, employee stock options cannot be exercised until they vest. After vesting, those options moving from out-of-the-money to in-the-money will have a longer duration than those options that are in-the-money at the time of vesting. A second resource, as discussed above, is the financial statements of public companies that provide information on the expected holding period of employee stock options they have issued. Finally, academic surveys and theoretical literature provide insight into expected holding periods.

E. VOLATILITY

Employee stock option value is impacted by the estimate of the expected volatility of the underlying security returns during the time to exercise (holding period). Volatility is measured by estimating the standard deviation of security returns that likely will occur in the future. This typically is accomplished by analyzing the historical standard deviation of returns. As illustrated in Table 2-7 below, the share price for Stock A has ranged from $22 per share to $25 during the past four months, resulting in a standard deviation of returns equaling 14.8%.[15]

Table 2-7
Share Price Volatility

Time Period	Share Price: Stock A	Monthly Return
Current Month	$ 25.00	13.6%
Last Month	$ 22.00	-12.0%
Two Months Ago	$25.00	13.6%
Three Months Ago	$ 22.00	
Standard Deviation of Returns		14.8%
Time Period	Share Price: Stock B	Monthly Return
Current Month	$32.00	45.5%
Last Month	$22.00	-31.3%
Two Months Ago	$25.00	45.5%
Three Months Ago	$22.00	
Standard Deviation of Returns		44.3%

Stock B has ranged in price from $22 to $32 per share. The returns of Stock B are more volatile in that they exhibit a greater range of outcomes. This results in the returns of Stock B having a larger standard deviation than the returns of Stock A. Based upon history, the share price of Stock B will be more volatile than that of Stock A, providing the option investor more upside potential for gain. As previously discussed, the greater downside potential is not relevant for the option investor.

In addition, the longer the expected duration of the option, the greater volatility's impact on value. The impact of a change in expected volatility is shown below using Johnson & Johnson employee stock options granted in 2004. Johnson & Johnson financial statements report an option value of $13.11 using an expected life of five years and a 27% volatility factor. As shown on Table 2-8 below, increasing the expected volatility of Johnson & Johnson stock returns from 27% to 100% increases the value of their options from $13.11 to $49.27.

Table 2-8
Impact of Changing Volatility

Johnson & Johnson Corporation

Volatility	Option Value
27%	$ 13.11
50%	$ 22.03
75%	$ 30.38
100%	$ 49.27

An expected volatility of 100% is not uncommon for small public firms as well as firms in highly volatile industries such as biotechnology. As shown on Table 2-9, the stock options of Avanir, a biotechnology firm, have been valued using volatiles ranging from 95% to 133% over the past few years. In addition, volatility estimates change over time. As indicated, Intel lowered its expected volatility in 2004 from 50% to 30%.

Table 2-9
Volatility Utilized in Employee Stock Option Valuation

	2004	2003	2002
Johnson & Johnson Corporation	27.0%	28.0%	26.0%
Intel Corporation	30.0%	50.0%	50.0%
Avanir Pharmaceuticals, Inc.	95.0%	133.0%	125.0%

Avanir also lowered its expected volatility in 2004. Lower volatility reduces the value of employee stock options. All else being equal, firms generally will prefer to use the lower volatiles because the resulting lower option valuation reduces the impact of new accounting guidelines that require firms to expense stock options rather than simply disclose their value. Therefore, when valuation experts use financial statement volatility estimates, they should be validated.

The validation of estimated employee stock volatility can be accomplished by estimating the historical volatility of the underlying security. Whether a firm's historical performance can be used as a proxy for future performance is a difficult judgment. For example, if the stock market and the underlying stock returns have been abnormally stable or volatile, it may not be reasonable to assume such a condition will continue into the future. However, as a firm matures, its stock return volatility generally decreases.

An analysis of historical volatility can often be complemented by determining the volatility of a company's publicly traded options. This is achieved by finding the volatility that is consistent with the traded value of a company's traded stock options. For example, short-term traded options often will have different volatilities than traded long-term options. Even here judgment must be applied as imputed volatility will change with option characteristics. The analysis of volatilities used by comparable companies can also provide valuable insights.

F. ARE VALUES DETERMINED BY THE BSOPM TOO OVERLY SPECULATIVE TO BE USED FOR EQUITABLE DISTRIBUTION?

In contrast to the accounting profession, the SEC, the IRS, and some courts have been reluctant to use the BSOPM to value executive stock options. Courts that have rejected the BSOPM as a tool in evaluating employee stock options for equitable distribution purposes base their reluctance on the notion that the BSOPM provides a value that is no more than a "mere expectancy."[16]

Although we agree with the court that it is impossible to know what a stock will be worth on any future date, it is not the case that the current value of a vested or unvested employee stock option cannot be measured with reasonable accuracy. For example, assume that an employee has Johnson & Johnson employee stock options identical to the traded out-of-the money options (see Table 2-6). Does the lack of marketability that makes their value unrealizable at any given point in time make the option value so speculative that their value to the employee cannot be measured? We do not believe so. The lack of marketability will reduce value, but it does not make common sense that the traded Johnson & Johnson option that has market value of $6.15 has no value for purposes of equitable distribution.

In 1995, the accounting profession formally recognized in Statement of Financial Accounting Standards No. 123 (SFAS 123) that executive stock options have an ascertainable value beyond their intrinsic value.[17] In addition, the BSOPM was recognized as an appropriate method to calculate the value of executive stock options by the accounting profession as reprinted here:

> The Board's conclusion that recognizing the costs of all stock-based employee compensation, including fixed, at-the-money stock options, is the preferable accounting method stems from the following premises:
>
> a. Employee stock options have value.
> b. Valuable financial instruments given to employees give rise to compensation cost that is properly included in measuring an entity's net income.
> c. The value of employee stock options can be estimated within acceptable limits for recognition in financial statements.[18]

SFAS 123 stated further that:

> An employee stock option has value when it is granted regardless of whether, ultimately, (a) the employee exercises the option and purchases stock worth more than the employee pays for it or (b) the option expires worthless at the end of the option period.[19]

Finally, SFAS 123 provided that:

> The fair value of a stock option (or its equivalent) granted by a public entity shall be estimated using an option-pricing model (for example, the Black-Scholes or a **binomial model**) that takes into account as of the grant date the exercise price and expected life of the option, the current price of the underlying stock and its expected volatility, expected dividends on the stock (except as provided in paragraphs 32 and 33), and the risk-free interest rate for the expected term of the option.[20]

SFAS 123 was revised in 2004 and now requires firms to recognize option expense calculated by option pricing models such as the BSOPM in their financial statements rather than simply disclose them.[21] This provides further evidence that option values can be determined with reasonable accuracy.

In addition, the disclosure format adopted by the SEC for long-term options issued to executives explicitly includes information on the value of granted executive stock options. As stated by the SEC, "As an alternative to use of hypothetical values, presentation of grant-date option values calculated through use of a recognized valuation formula, such as the "Black-Scholes" option-pricing model, will be permitted."

In Rev. Proc. 98-34,[22] the IRS adopted the BSOPM as an appropriate valuation methodology when determining the value of executive stock options for gift and estate tax valuations. It is worth noting that marketability discounts are not permitted to account for the lack of transferability of executive stock options. The reduction in value is captured through using the option's expected time to exercise, not the time to expiration. The adoption of the BSOPM by the IRS is significant in that the methodology analysts use to value closely held businesses for equitable distribution also flow from IRS revenue rulings geared toward estate and tax valuations. In *Davidson v. Davidson*,[23] the court adopted the BSOPM model based upon the accounting profession adoption of the BSOPM.

In summary, most regulatory agencies, academics, investors, and accounting professionals agree that employee stock options can be valued using employee option pricing models with reasonable accuracy for decision making and financial statement disclosure. In contrast, equitable distribution courts generally have held that employee stock option value estimates are too speculative to be of use.

G. MARKETABILITY ISSUES POST EMPLOYEE STOCK OPTION EXERCISE[24]

As noted above, a reduction in option value based upon early exercise accounts for the lack of marketability in employee stock options. Therefore, no additional discount from value is appropriate. However, some employees are not free to sell their shares after they have exercised their employee stock options. This can occur because they are senior executives who can only trade at certain times during the year, or the option plan places restrictions on when shares can be sold after exercise. In this situation, a marketability discount in the range of 2% to 10% often is appropriate.

A marketability discount may also be warranted for employees who receive restricted stock as part of their compensation package. Restricted stock is stock that is not readily tradable. It is issued for any number of reasons, including raising funds for capital projects and as part of executive compensation plans. Typically, restricted stock is offered at a discount from its publicly traded counterpart. The generally accepted inference is that the discount reflects compensation for a lack of liquidity. That is, the holder of the restricted stock cannot sell the asset and gain the cash flow, and when the restriction period is over, may not be able to sell the asset close to the original price of the unrestricted stock.

Over the past several years, the literature on observed restricted stock discounts through private placement discounts has evolved. Observed discounts between the price of the restricted stock issue through a private placement and their freely traded counterparts are no longer viewed as solely reflective of marketability discounts. Hertzel and Smith[25] postulated that observed discounts of restricted stock might not represent a marketability discount. Their sample included 106 private placements announcements made between 1980 and May 1987. Regression analysis indicated that the difference between restricted share (unregistered) prices and freely traded (registered) share prices in private placement were 13.5% after consideration of firm performance and other factors such as buyer characteristics. They conclude that even a 13.5% discount may overstate the pure marketability discount.

Bajaj, Denis, Ferris, and Sarin[26] also have studied discounts associated with private placements of publicly traded securities and have concluded that historical discounts of 35% are probably overstated. They also refer to the possibility of zero cost collars as a mechanism to restore marketability. Their analysis of 88 private placements taking place between 1990 and 1995 indicate that private placement of registered (freely traded shares) were issued at a median discount of 9.85%, whereas unregistered (restricted shares) were issued at a median discount of 26.47%. The discount for registered shares cannot be related to marketability because these shares are freely traded. A regression analysis was performed to control for the financial performance of the firms issuing registered and unregistered securities. They conclude that a marketability discount of approximately 7% is appropriate. The engineering of an at-the-money equity collar ("**collar**") offers the valuation professional a direct means to calculate an appropriate discount. Such a collar removes the price risk inherent in restricted stock holdings. This process is demonstrated in Table 2-10 using publicly traded Target Corporation options.

H. DETERMINING AN APPROPRIATE MARKETABILITY DISCOUNT

When an employee holds restricted stock the consequences resulting from a lack of marketability can be eliminated through an at-the-money equity collar. An at-the-money collar is constructed by selling calls and purchasing puts with an exercise price equal to the current share price of the underlying security. The collar creates a perfect hedge resulting in the investor receiving 100% of the value of the underlying security at the date the collar is created at the expiration date of the collar. Thus, all price risk is eliminated. Table 2-10 shows actual options trading data for Target Corporation put and call options on February 20, 2004 (February 19, 2004 closing data). Target closed at a price of $42.16. **Open interest** tells how many option contracts are in force on January 30, 2004. Each contract represents options on 100 shares. Thus, there are 552,100 call options outstanding on Target Corporation stock with a strike price of $40.00 that expire on January 21, 2005.

Table 2-10
Target Corporation Traded Options

February 20, 2004 (Closing Price February 19, 2004) Closing Share Price $ 42.15			
	Strike Price	Average of Bid-Ask Spread	Open Interest
Call Options Expiring January 21, 2005	$ 40.00 $ 45.00	$ 5.65 $ 3.10	5,521 2,774
Put Options Expiring January 21, 2005	$ 40.00 $ 45.00	$ 3.25 $ 5.70	1,298 387

An at-the-money-equity collar is constructed by writing calls, thus receiving the call premium as well as purchasing put options at the same exercise price. The call writer receives a call premium. In return, the call writer must deliver shares of stock at the strike price. In the above example, the call writer receives $5.65 for agreeing to deliver a share of Target stock for a purchase price of $40.00.

The purchaser of a put pays a put premium and then has the right to sell stock at the strike price. In the above example, by paying a put premium of $3.25, an investor has the right to sell one share of Target at a price of $40.00 through the expiration date. By combining writing calls and purchasing puts one can eliminate the risk of share price fluctuations.

Assume we wish to collar the value of 10,000 shares of Target Corporation stock. This will require us to engineer 100 equity collars. Engineering 57 collars with an exercise price of $40 and 43 collars with an exercise price of $45.00 will create an equity collar for Target Corporation with an average exercise share price of $42.15, which is Target's closing share price on the day the collars are engineered.

When the collar expires on January 21, 2005, the investor will have locked in the February 20, 2004 share price of $42.15. For example, assume the share price falls to $35 per share when the option expires. Buyers of the call will not exercise the option to buy shares; however, the investor creating the collar will exercise the puts that allows shares to be sold at their exercise price of $40.00 and $45.00 and receive the average price of $42.15.

If Target's share price increases to over $45 per share on January 21, 2005, the puts will expire with no value and the investor creating the hedge delivers the shares to the buyer at an average call exercise price of $42.15. Again, the investor engineering the collar will receive exactly $42.15 per share when the options expire.

In summary, the at-the-money equity collar has eliminated all price risk. The cost of eliminating price risk represents one component of the marketability discount. The transactions cost of creating such a collar typically is 1% to 3% of dollar value collared. The precise net transaction cost for engineering an equity collar depends upon the number of collars created, the put-call spread, and transaction cost for executing the transaction.

Although the equity collar eliminates price risk, it does not provide immediate access to funds, thus liquidity is lost for the duration of the collar. In situations where restricted stock are valued for purposes of equitable distribution, a cash equivalent value can be determined by increasing the marketability discount for the forgone interest on the funds collared. The advantage of the equity collar to calculate appropriate discount is that it provides a more direct and definitive calculation for a given set of circumstances.

I. SUMMARY AND CONCLUSION

Employee stock options generally have significant value, although their lack of transferability may result in unrealizable value at any given point in time. The accounting profession, the SEC, the IRS, and the academic community have all decided that employee stock options can be valued with reasonable accuracy. Ultimately, employee stock option values are determined by the same variables that determine publicly traded option values. The value of an employee stock option as determined by modern option pricing models takes into account that future share prices cannot be known with certainty. The family lawyer should feel confident that financial experts are capable of assessing employee stock option values.

Notes
1. This discussion limited to call options. Options that allow an investor to sell shares of stock at a fixed price are known as put options.
2. Option valuation using complex decision trees are called lattice models. Lattice models are now being used by many firms to determine the value of employee stock options in their financial statements. *See* Lester Barenbaum et al., *Valuing Employee Stock Options Using a Lattice Model,*

THE CPA JOURNAL, Dec. 2004, at 16–20. Portions of the material in this section are adapted with permission.

3. Fisher Black had passed away by 1997, and Nobel Prizes are not awarded posthumously.

4. The material in this section is adapted with permission from NEW JERSEY FAMILY LAW PRACTICE, 9th ed., chap. 13 (New Jersey Institute for Continuing Legal Education 1999).

5. Nalin Kulatilaka & Alan Marcus, *Valuing Employee Stock Options*, FIN. ANALYSIS J. (Nov./Dec. 1994), at 46–56.

6. *Id*. at 54.

7. *See* S. Huddart, *Employee Stock Options*, J. ACCT. & ECON. (1994), at 207–31.

8. *Id*. at 220.

9. Jennifer Carpenter, *The Exercise and Valuation of Executive Stock Options,* J. FIN. ECON. (1998), at 127–58.

10. *Id*. at 154.

11. *See* S. Huddart & M. Lang, *Employee Stock Option Exercises: An Empirical Analysis,* 21 J. ACCT. & ECON. (1996), at 5–43.

12. Carpenter, *supra* note 9.

13. Statement of Fin. Accounting Standards No. 123R (FASB 2004), ¶ A26 (emphasis added).

14. Johnson & Johnson Form 10-K for the period ending Jan. 2, 2005, at 47–49.

15. See Appendix 2-A, *infra*, for a short discussion of how to interpret and calculate standard deviation.

16. *See, e.g.,* Wendt v. Wendt, D.N. FA 960149562S, CN. Super. (1998).

17. ACCOUNTING FOR STOCK-BASED COMPENSATION, Statement of Fin. Accounting Standards No. 123 (Fin. Accounting Standards Bd. 1995).

18. *Id*. at ¶ 75.

19. *Id*. at ¶ 78.

20. *Id*. at ¶ 19 (emphasis added).

21. SHARE-BASED PAYMENT, Statement of Accounting Standards No. 123 (Fin. Accounting Standards Bd. 2004).

22. Rev. Proc. 98-34, 1998-17 I.R.B. 15.

23. 578 N.W.2d 848 (Neb. 1998).

24. The material in this section is drawn from Lester Barenbaum & Walter Schubert, *Modern Financial Engineering and Discounts: The Collar Message*, BUS. VALUATION REV. (Mar. 2004), at 69–73. Adapted with permission from the Business Valuation Committee of the American Society of Appraisers.

25. M. Hertzel & R. Smith, *Market Discounts and Shareholder Gains for Placing Equity Privately*, J. FIN. (June 1993), at 459–85.

26. M. Bajaj, D. Denis, S. Ferris & A. Sarin, *The Value of Resale Limitations on Restricted Stock: An Option Theory Approach*, J. CORP. L. (Fall 2001), at 89–115.

Appendix 2-A
The Standard Deviation

Risk is commonly measured through the variation or volatility of expected outcome. The greater the variation in possible outcome, the more risky the event. For example, Investments A and B below both have an expected return of $100 one year from now. However, Investment B is riskier given its greater variation in expected outcome.

Expected Price Outcomes

Investment A	Probability of Outcome	Investment B
$90	1/5	$25
$95	1/5	$50
$100	1/5	$100
$105	1/5	$150
$110	1/5	$175
$100	**Expected Outcome**	**$100**

Volatility measurements attempt to give the investor an idea of the likelihood that the returns will be close to that which is expected. The greater the volatility or variation in outcomes, the greater the risk exposure borne by the investor.

The most popular measurement of volatility is standard deviation. The standard deviation measures the difference in outcomes from the average outcome. The methodology is to measure the mean of a sample of outcomes and measure the standard deviation around that mean. The way this is done is to take the difference between each actual outcome and the mean and square the difference. Squaring the difference eliminates the impact of negative values offsetting positive values. In fact, since it is the average that is calculated, the sum of the differences, if not squared, would equal zero. These squared differences are then added together and divided by the number of observations less one. The square root of that value is then calculated. By taking the square root, the value is returned to the same units as the original measurement.

For example, imagine an investor wants to measure the volatility of the outcomes of Investment A and Investment B. First, the expected or mean expected outcome must be determined. As shown above, the expected outcome for both Investments A and B is $100.

The investor then calculates the variation around the mean outcome by taking each expected outcome and subtracting it from the mean outcome and squaring the results, as shown below.

Calculation of Standard Deviation

90 – 100 = –10	100.00
95 – 100 = –5	25.00
100 – 100 = 0	-
105 – 100 = 5	25.00
110 – 100 = 10	100.00
Sum of Squared Differences	250.00
Divided by 4	62.50
Square Root = Standard Deviation of Investment A Outcomes	**$ 7.91**

The investor performs this calculation for each observation and then sums the values that total 250.00 as shown. Next, the investor divides that sum by four, which represent the five observations less one. The square root of 62.50 is $7.91, which is the standard deviation of the expected outcomes. This means that the observations tend to cluster around plus or minus $7.91 from the expected mean outcome of $100. In contrast, the standard deviation is $31.60 for Investment B. The standard deviation of $31.60 for Investment B quantifies that the variation of outcomes for Investment B is greater than Investment A, indicating Investment B's greater risk.

When measuring the volatility of securities, using returns rather than stock price is preferable. For example, imagine an investor purchases a share of stock for $100 on March 30. On April 30 the stock had a value of $110; on May 30 $95; on June 30 $105; and on July 30 $120. The average value of the stock would have been $106 and the standard deviation would have been $9.61. Alternatively, imagine that the stock costs $10 on March 30 (because the investor invested $100, the investor would have purchased 10 shares). On April 30 the stock was at $11; on May 30 at $9.50; on June 30 $10.50; and on July 30 $12.00. The average value of the stock would be $10.60 and the standard deviation would be calculated to be $.96. Note that the volatility of the first investment was far greater than the second. However, having purchased ten shares, the investor's portfolio position is exactly the same as in the first case. In both cases, the returns were as follows: for the month ending on April 30 the return was 10%, for the month ending May 30 the return was -13.6%; for the month ending June 30 the return was 10.5%; and for the month ending July 30 the return was 12.0%. In sum, measuring asset volatility by employing rates of return better measures the change in capital or portfolio value, and therefore is favored. In both cases, the average return was 5.3% and the standard deviation was 12.75%.

Option value is impacted differently by volatility than the value of most other assets. From the perspective of most investors, volatility creates a negative impact on their investment choice. Given any specific expected return and faced with increased risk, an investor will wish to pay less for an asset. However, such is not the case when options are considered. An option gives an investor the right but not the obligation to purchase or sell a specified asset over or at a specified period of time. The investor is not forced to purchase or sell. For example, assume an employee is granted stock options to purchase his or her company's stock for $40.00 per share. If the stock is at $40.00 or less, the employee will not exercise the option. It makes no difference what the price is if it is $40.00 or less. The employee loses no more at $3.00 than at $40.00. That is, if the option matures out of the money, the employee receives nothing. However, upside potential is a different story. It makes a big difference if the stock is $40.25 or $75.00. Therefore, upside volatility is very important to the employee, but downside volatility is not. Thus, volatility is good for an option holder and creates value in an option.

Assume that an employee is awarded stock options that can be exercised at the current market price of $50.00. Further assume that returns on the stock are log normally distributed (meaning that the constantly compounded returns on the stock are normally distributed). If the standard deviation were 20%, then there was a 68% chance that the stock price would rise or fall at a fully compounded rate of 20% or less. That is, there is a 68% chance that the actual stock price at the end of the year will be between $40.94 and $61.07. If the standard deviation were 40%, there would be a 68% chance that the stock value would lay between $74.59 and $33.52. The upside potential grows but the downside potential is irrelevant. In sum, the greater the measured standard deviation of an option, the more valuable the option.

Taxation of Employee Stock Options, Restricted Stock, and Stock Appreciation Rights*

3

A. INTRODUCTION

The employee tax liability resulting from the exercise of employee stock options is an important factor that family law practitioners must address as part of the property settlement in a divorce. In this chapter, we examine the tax treatment of both nonqualified stock options and incentive stock options. New revenue rulings are discussed with examples. In addition, the tax impact of employee stock options as it relates to marital settlements is examined.

The taxation of compensation depends upon the type of stock option exercised by the employee. Stock options come in two forms: statutory options, commonly termed **incentive stock options** (ISOs) and nonstatutory options, commonly termed **nonqualified stock options** (NQSOs). The Internal Revenue Code provides ISOs with very favorable tax treatment.[1] However, this favorable treatment comes with a price. If certain qualifications are met, the options are deemed to be statutory, providing the employee with significant tax benefits.[2] This serves as a great incentive to the employees receiving the options. The quid

---

* Jack Zook, CPA, PFS, MBA, is the primary author of this chapter. Jack is an Assistant Professor of Accounting at La Salle University and a Managing Director at Zook, Dinon & Roman, P.A., Moorestown, New Jersey.

pro quo here is the employer who granted the option receives no compensation deduction in these options transactions.[3] The nonqualified stock option usually results in ordinary income to the employee, generally at the exercise date[4] and produces a compensation deduction at the same time for the employer.[5]

The key chapter points listed below provides a tax checklist that family law practitioners can utilize when assessing the tax consequences of employee stock options as part of a marital estate.

- Determine whether the employee stock options under analysis are transferable to family members as part of a divorce. New revenue rulings allow tax free transfers of employee stock options as part of an equitable distribution agreement. Such transfers can be very beneficial when the tax rates of the parties are materially different.
- Determine whether the timing of employee stock option exercise during a given year under a constructive trust agreement may impact the employment taxes paid by the titled spouse.
- Marital agreements should be drafted with explicit language in regard to how the parties will share the tax burden of employee stock options. This should include references to federal income taxes, local and state income taxes, and employment taxes.
- Marital agreements should be clear whether any tax burden will be based upon the parties average tax rate or marginal taxes due. Marginal taxes due should be based on the overall tax liability calculated with and without the exercise of options.

B. TAX ASPECTS OF NONQUALIFIED STOCK OPTIONS

The taxation of nonqualified stock options is materially different from that of incentive stock options. As part of discovery it is important to determine whether granted options are nonqualified or incentive stock options (qualified). This information generally is stated on the annual option statement issued to the employee each year.

NQSOs can be taxed either to the employee at the **grant date** or the exercise date. The factor that determines which date is to be used depends upon whether a readily ascertainable fair market value can be established. If market value is ascertainable at the grant date, then the employee (grantee) will recognize compensation to the extent of the fair market value of the stock options.[6] The employer corporation (grantor) recognizes as a compensation deduction of the same amount and in the same year as the employee recognizes it as income.[7] Once this income recognition takes place, the compensation part of the process is completed. If the employee would subsequently exercise those options, no compensation would be recognized as a result.[8] Nonqualified stock options infrequently have readily ascertainable fair market values. In general, for a NQSO to have a readily ascertainable value it must have all the following attributes:

a) vested and free of restrictions;
b) transferable by the discretion of the employee; and
c) a readily ascertainable fair market value.

Unvested options by definition do not have a readily ascertainable market value. However, even vested options may not have an ascertainable market value if they are encumbered by any number of restrictions, such as forfeiture risk as part of an employee's employment agreement. Firms may allow ISOs and NQSOs to be transferable to family members and estate tax vehicles. This limited transferability does not meet the transferability threshold above. As yet, financial disclosures on a firm's financial statements providing estimates of employee stock option values have not been used to provide a readily ascertainable fair market value.

Because the above conditions are rarely met, NQSO taxation generally occurs only upon exercise. Correspondingly, the employer will not be allowed any compensation deduction until the exercise of the NQSO, and the employee typically is not taxed at grant.

The key date for the tax impact now shifts to the exercise date. When the employee exercises the stock option, the compensation to the employee equals the excess, if any, of the fair market value of the stock on the exercise date over the exercise price paid. The employee recognizes this so-called bargain element as ordinary income.[9] The employer corporation (grantor) recognizes as a compensation deduction in the same amount and in the same year as the employee recognizes the income.[10] This completes the compensation part of the process. As the employee sells the stock obtained through the exercise, capital gain (or loss) will result at those future dates. We will now review each step of the process through examples that illustrate the specific provisions and significant dates.

C. TAXATION AT THE DATE OF GRANT

When the fair market value of a nonstatutory (nonqualified) stock option is not readily ascertainable at the grant date, then no compensation results to the employee at that point in time.[11] The employer is not entitled to any deduction for compensation and no basis arises in the options at that time. As was stated above, determining a readily ascertainable fair market value at the grant date rarely happens.

Example 1: No Readily Ascertainable Fair Market Value at Grant Date

On January 2, 1998, C Corporation ("C") grants to employee E ("E"), for services rendered, an option to purchase 1,000 shares of stock. The option may be exercised in whole or in part over the next 5 years. The exercise price is $10 per share and the fair market value of C's stock is $5 per share. Because the stock option has no readily ascertainable fair market value at the grant date, no compensation results to E and no tax deduction arises for C.

Tax Consequences:

Ordinary compensation to E in 1998:	None
Ordinary compensation deduction to C in 1998:	None

D. TAXATION AT THE EXERCISE DATE

When the market value of the stock rises above the exercise price, the employee likely will exercise the option. Assuming the employee exercises the option, the employee recognizes compensation income to the extent of the excess of the fair market value of the stock over the exercise price.[12] This compensation income will be included in the employee's W-2 and taxed as ordinary income at the regular tax rates (10%–35%). At the same time, the employer takes a compensation deduction equal to the amount of compensation recognized by the employee.[13] The basis of the newly acquired stock will equal the sum of the amount of compensation recognized by the employee and the amount of the exercise price paid. Both of these components determine the basis.

Example 2: Compensation Determined at Exercise Date

On January 2, 2001, when C's stock has a fair market value of $30 per share, E exercises his option at $10 per share for 1,000 shares and pays C $10,000. E recognizes compensation of $20 per share, or $20,000 in total. C will take a deduction for the $20,000 in its corporate return for 2001. The basis in the stock will be the amount paid for the exercise and the compensation income recognized by E.

Tax Consequences:

Ordinary compensation to E in 2001:	$20,000
Ordinary compensation deduction to C in 2001:	$20,000
Basis in 1,000 shares of stock*	$30,000
Holding period for the stock begins the day after the option is exercised	January 3, 2001

Note: The basis in the stock consists of the amount of compensation recognized by E upon exercise of the option and the payment made by E to C when the option is exercised.

Upon subsequent disposition of the stock, the employee recognizes a capital gain or loss equal to the difference between the basis and the proceeds from the sale of the stock. The holding period will determine short-term or long-term treatment of the resulting capital gain or loss. Current tax regulations require that after exercise the security must be held for one year to receive capital gains treatment.

Example 3: Stock Sold; Disposition of Stock

On January 2, 2003, when the market price of the stock is $75 per share, E sells all 1,000 shares for total proceeds of $75,000.

Tax Consequences:

Ordinary compensation to E in 2003:	None
Ordinary compensation deduction to C in 2003:	None
Long-term capital gain*	$45,000

Note: The holding period began the date after the exercise of the option, January 3, 2001. Because the holding period exceeded one year, the capital gain or loss is long-term and subject to the maximum capital gains rates of 5% or 15%, depending on E's regular tax bracket. The $45,000 gain represents the excess of the total proceeds realized less stock basis ($75,000–$30,000).

Example 4: Option Goes Unexercised; Option Expires Out-of-the-Money

If the employee fails to exercise his or her options or the options expire, then the employee will not recognize any compensation and there will be no gain or loss on the expiration. No taxable income consequences arise.

On January 2, 2004, C's stock price is $5 per share. E fails to exercise his option within the five-year period and it expires worthless.

Tax Consequences:

Ordinary compensation to E in 2004:	None
Ordinary compensation deduction to C in 2004:	None
Long-term capital loss for E*	None

Note: Upon expiration of the option, E has no gain or loss of any kind because there was no compensation recognized by E, nor was there any payment to C for the exercise of the option.

E. MARITAL PROPERTY SETTLEMENTS AND NONSTATUTORY STOCK OPTIONS

Some companies allow NQSOs to be transferred to a spouse as part of the marital property settlement. The Securities and Exchange Commission amended its rules in 1999 to facilitate such a transfer.[14] When such a transfer takes place, the income tax consequence will be based upon the tax status of the nontitled spouse rather than the titled spouse. When the marginal tax rates of the titled and nontitled spouse is different, it will be worthwhile to ascertain whether the titled spouse's firm will allow unexercised NQSOs to be transferred to the nontitled spouse.

Even if a firm's stock option plan does not allow transfers for a divorce settlement, constructive trusts can be drawn that allow the nontitled spouse to instruct the titled spouse to exercise options on his or her behalf. As discussed below, the tax consequences of the exercise of NQSOs have been clarified by several recent revenue rulings.

Transfer of property in divorce generally does not result in income to either spouse.[15] In Rev. Rul. 2002-22,[16] the IRS ruled that the employee who was granted nonqualified stock options did not recognize income at the grant date because the options did not have a readily ascertainable fair market value. As a result of the marital settlement, the employee-spouse transferred one-third of the NQSOs to the former spouse. Consistent with marital property settlements, the transferee spouse does not recognize income on the transfer of those options. However, the transferee spouse, not the transferor spouse, will recognize income when he or she exercises the stock options (just as the employee would have recognized income had the stock options remained the employee's property). When the transferee spouse exercises the stock options, ordinary income will result just as if the transferee spouse had performed the services. Federal income tax should be withheld on this income.

Subsequently, the IRS issued Rev. Rul. 2004-60,[17] which restates the same fact pattern in Rev. Rul. 2002-22, and extends it to describe the employment tax consequences related to the marital settlement of nonstatutory stock options. Although the federal income tax consequences remain the same for the transferee former spouse, the transferor spouse is responsible for federal employment taxes when the compensation is recognized upon exercise. The employee who recognizes the federal employment taxes is able to take into account the other wages in that calendar year that have been subject to the Social Security wage base. The example below explains this scenario.

Example 5: Social Security Wage Base

The marital settlement requires employee H to transfer 1,000 nonstatutory stock options of corporation C to former spouse W. The options have an exercise price of $10. Because the nonstatutory stock options had no readily ascertainable fair market value at grant date, H previously recognized no ordinary income when C granted the options.

Assuming C's stock price rises to $35 per share and W decides to exercise the option, W would then recognize as ordinary income $25,000, which represents the difference between the exercise price and the fair market value of the stock ($35,000-$10,000). In effect, W steps into the shoes of employee H for federal income tax purposes. This reflects the position of Rev. Rul. 2002-22.

Rev. Rul. 2004-60 requires C to report to the transferee spouse the ordinary compensation and related federal tax withheld on Form 1099-MISC (to be received by W). Therefore, ordinary income of $25,000 and any federal income tax withheld will be reported to the IRS and W. C would recognize a compensation deduction of $25,000 in the same year.

However, employee H, the transferor, will be required to pay the applicable Social Security and Medicare tax on the amount of the compensation recognized by W, the transferee spouse. If H's other wages (which have been taken into account when the exercise occurs) do not exceed the Social Security base (formally known as the old-age, survivors, and disability insurance base), then 6.2%[18] should be paid by H on the compensation ($1,550 = $25,000 x 6.2%). In addition, H would also be responsible for the Medicare tax on this compensation ($362.50 = $25,000 x 1.45%).[19] There is no wage base limit for the Medicare tax. (NOTE: The maximum earnings subject to the Social Security tax will increase to $90,000 in calendar year 2005).

If H's other wages exceed the Social Security base when the exercise occurs, then H need only be responsible for the Medicare tax. In this example, H would save the $1,550. C is required to report the income recognized by W on H's W-2 as Social Security wages and related taxes withheld (if applicable) and Medicare wages and related taxes withheld in the year of exercise.

Example of Revenue Ruling 2002-22 and 2004-60
- Dick and Jane are divorced with Dick receiving stock options from Jane.
- Jane is in the 35 percent tax bracket and Dick is in the 20 percent tax bracket.
- Dick received 10,000 options with a strike or exercise price of $5.00 per share through an allowable transfer of options from Jane.
- Dick decides to exercise and sell via a **cashless exercise** when the stock is trading at $15.00 per share.
- Assume the maximum earnings subject to FICA (6.2 percent rate) is $90,000 and Medicare taxes are still at 1.45 percent on unlimited income.
- There are no state and local taxes in this example.

Scenario:
A) Dick (nontitled spouse) exercises options early in the year.
B) Dick exercises options after Jane's (titled spouse) income exceeds $90,000.

Scenarios	A	B
Option Proceeds (10,000 * $15)	150,000	150,000
Strike Price $5	50,000	50,000
Cashless Exercise Proceeds	100,000	100,000
Income Tax	20,000	20,000
FICA Tax (6.2% up to $90,000)	5,580	0
Medicare Taxes (1.45%)	1,450	1,450
Net Proceeds to Dick	**72,970**	**78,550**
Benefit of Timing		**5,580**

An issue arises of which spouse ultimately will bear the burden of the $5,580 of FICA taxes. In the above example, if Jane's (titled spouse) base salary was going to exceed $90,000, then a reasonable argument can be made that Dick (nontitled spouse) not bear the burden of any FICA taxes paid by Jane through an option exercise early in the year.

The transferee spouse's actions regarding the exercise of the options may have an adverse employment tax effect on the transferor spouse if the timing of the exercise is not done in conjunction with an analysis of the transferor spouse's calendar wage status. Timing of the exercise also should be evaluated from a multiple-tax-year perspective. If the transferor spouse anticipates his or her compensation in one year will exceed the Social Security wage base, then it would be beneficial to have the transferee spouse exercise the options in that year and subject the employee-spouse to only the Medicare tax on the compensation from the option exercise. In contrast, if the transferor spouse anticipates compensation totaling less than the Social Security wage base, then deferring the exercise of those options by the transferee spouse to another year would relieve the transferor spouse from having to pay some or all of the Social Security tax on the compensation from the exercise.

Given the above the possibilities, the marital property settlement must be clear on how the tax consequences of exercising employee stock options are to be shared. For example, if options are not transferred and a constructive trust agreement is utilized, then it should be made explicit how income taxes and employment taxes are to be shared.

Typically, both employment and income taxes are shared based upon the difference in taxes due before and after the exercise of stock options in any given taxable period.

F. TAX ASPECTS OF INCENTIVE STOCK OPTIONS

Incentive stock options, as they stand today, were a result of the Economic Recovery Tax Act of 1981.[20] Congress created this incentive-based vehicle to allow employers to use them as a tax-favored form of compensation. The employee has no tax consequences from the grant of an incentive stock option and no ordinary income tax.[21] To make them tax neutral, Congress did not allow the employing companies to take any tax deduction for the value of the statutory (qualified) options.[22]

An incentive stock option is subject to certain plan and employer requirements.[23] Those employer requirements are not relevant to our discussion here. What is relevant are the following two employee requirements to abide by certain terms for the option to remain qualified. The two key employee requirements are: 1) the employee must be employed by the issuing company at all times beginning on the grant date and ending on the day three months before the exercise date; and 2) the employee must not dispose of the stock within two years from the date of granting the option nor within one year after the option's exercise date.[24] The three-month window is extended to 12 months in cases of total and permanent disability of the employee and does not apply to exercises by an executor, administrator, or representative after an employee's death.

If there were a failure to meet any of the holding period requirements, the qualified option becomes a nonqualified option (a "disqualifying disposition") described above, and the stock options would then be governed by I.R.C. § 83.[25] Consider the three key dates—the grant date, exercise date and disposition date—and the related tax consequences of incentive stock options.

Grant Date

At the grant date, there is no compensation recognized by the employee.

Example 6: Grant Date
On January 2, 1999, corporation C grants to employee E an incentive stock option, the terms of which allow employee E the option to purchase 1,000 shares of C's stock for $25 per share over the next five years. The fair market value of C's stock is $30 at the date

of the grant. E recognizes no compensation at the grant date. The stock options have no basis because E did not recognize any compensation at this time, and E has not yet exercised the options. C is not entitled to any deduction at this or any other date.

Tax Consequences:

Ordinary compensation to E in 1999:	None
Ordinary compensation deduction to C in 1999:	None
E's basis in options	None

Once granted, E must observe the holding period rules discussed earlier to derive the tax benefits incentive stock options can provide. Violation of these holding period rules will result in the stock options receiving NQSO tax treatment.

Exercise Date

At the exercise date, there is no compensation recognized by the employee and no tax deduction by the employer.[26] At this point, however, there may be alternative minimum tax consequences, which is discussed at section H, *infra*. Upon exercise, the employee established the basis of the stock as the amount paid.

Example 7: Exercise Date

On January 3, 2001, the market price of C's stock is $75 per share. Employee E exercises the stock option and pays C $25,000 for 1,000 shares. E does not recognize any compensation at the date of exercise. The $50,000 benefit (market value of $75,000 less cost to exercise of $25,000) is not recognized by E as ordinary income or capital gain. E's basis in the stock is $25,000.

Tax Consequences:

Ordinary compensation to E in 2001:	None
Ordinary compensation deduction to C in 2001:	None
Basis in 1,000 shares of stock*	$25,000

Note: The basis in the stock consists of the payment made by E to C when the option is exercised.

Typically, when incentive stock options are exercised, the underlying stock also is sold. Disposing of the stock at the time of exercise provides the option holder the cash for the exercise and for the tax liability. Any gains on the disposition of the stock will be taxed at ordinary income tax rates because the holding period for capital gains treatment will not be met. However, if E decides not to dispose of the stock at the time of exercise, the benefit of the market value in excess of the exercise price is an item for adjustment for alternative minimum tax purposes and may result in E having to pay the alternative minimum tax.[27] The holding period rules require the stock to be held for more than one year after the date the option was exercised.[28] Assuming the holding period is observed, the amount realized is compared to the basis of the stock when the stock is disposed, and a long-term capital gain or loss will result.

Disposition Date

Example 8: Disposition Date

On January 2, 2003, when the market price of the stock is $100 per share, E sells all 1,000 shares for total proceeds of $100,000.

Tax Consequences:

Ordinary compensation to E in 2003:	None
Ordinary compensation deduction to C in 2003:	None
Long-term capital gain*:	$75,000

*Note: The holding period began the date after the exercise of the option: January 3, 2001. Because the holding period exceeded one year, the capital gain or loss is long term and subject to the maximum capital gains rates of 5% or 15%, depending on E's regular tax bracket. The $75,000 gain is derived from total proceeds realized less stock basis ($100,000-$50,000).

In essence, the employee was able to obtain long-term capital gain treatment upon the disposition of the stock obtained by way of the incentive stock options. There is no ordinary income recognized in this compensatory process. With the differential in tax rates between the highest regular income tax rate and long-term capital gains tax rate, a 20% federal tax savings resulted. The downside is that, unlike NQSOs, the employer receives no compensation deduction for the income recognized by the employee. It is easy to see why this has been such a powerful motivating tool for companies to use.

If E were to dispose of the stock within one year or less, the disposition would be considered a "disqualifying disposition" and would require E to recognize as compensation income the difference between the exercise price and the fair market value of the stock at the date of exercise. The recognition would occur in the year of the disqualifying disposition. C would also be entitled to a compensation deduction of the same amount in the same year.[29] The amount of compensation recognized would be added to the basis of the stock that was disposed, thus reducing the capital gain on the sale. In effect, these provisions convert potential long-term capital gain income into ordinary income and, accordingly, increase E's federal tax liability. Note that under I.R.C. § 421(b), the employer is not required to withhold income tax in the event of a disqualifying disposition. If the option is never exercised, then there is no tax consequence at all. It is as if it never happened.

Example 9: Option Expires
If E fails to exercise the stock options before the **expiration date**, then E recognizes no compensation in any form. C does not receive any compensation deduction for the expiring options because no basis in those options was established.

G. MARITAL PROPERTY SETTLEMENTS AND INCENTIVE STOCK OPTIONS

Following the treatment of NQSOs, marital transfers of stock resulting from the exercise of incentive stock options as part of the property settlement is not deemed to be a disposition and does not result in income to the recipient spouse. As a general rule, no gain or loss shall be recognized on a transfer of property from an individual to a former spouse.[30] The former spouse who receives the incentive stock options is afforded the same tax treatment that the employee-spouse would have had regarding a subsequent disposition of the stock.[31]

To prevent a disqualifying disposition from occurring, the former spouse must observe the same holding period for the stock as the employee-spouse. Failure to do so will result in ordinary compensation reported to the former spouse as opposed to potential long-term capital gain treatment.

The IRS issued a private letter ruling in 2005[32] stating that a constructive trust that allows the nontitled spouse to order the titled spouse to exercise incentive stock options and transfer the stock to the nontitled spouse does not violate the non-transferability of incentive stock option and will not result in a taxable event. When the stock is sold, the gain or loss will be recognized by the nontitled spouse. In addition, any alternative minimum taxable income resulting from the exercise of options will be included the nontitled spouse's income. Again, this new ruling may provide a benefit to the nontitled spouse if he or she has a lower marginal tax rate than the titled spouse.

H. ALTERNATIVE MINIMUM TAX

Although the exercise of an incentive stock option does not result in any ordinary income to the employee, it may have **alternative minimum tax (AMT)** implications. Assume the employee exercises the options when the market price of the stock exceeds the exercise price. This excess is an item of adjustment (also referred to as a "deferral item") for AMT calculations. As a result, the employee, although paying no regular tax on any ordinary income, may find him- or herself paying the AMT on this "phantom income."

Once the AMT is paid on this deferral item, it may be used as a tax credit in future years to offset the regular income tax liability when the gain arises from the disposition of the stock acquired from previously exercising the option. However, be aware that this AMT credit can only be used when the regular tax exceeds the total AMT, and *then* only to the extent that the regular tax exceeds the AMT. Consequently, this AMT credit may take years to utilize, if ever, depending on the circumstances. The AMT credit may be carried over indefinitely.

It is imperative that a tax professional review the status of such options before the end of the calendar year of exercise. If the market value of the stock at year-end drops below the market value at the date of exercise, it would be prudent to sell the shares, thus creating a disqualifying disposition to avoid paying the AMT. This is because the credit would be useless if the stock ultimately were sold at a price less than the value at the time of purchase. If the employee exercises the options and disposes of the stock in the same tax year, then the AMT adjustment is not needed because the "phantom income" now will be reported as a gain for both regular income tax and AMT purposes in the same year.

I. TAX ASPECTS OF STOCK APPRECIATION RIGHTS

Although stock options have provided corporations with an incentive level of compensation, they require the employee to utilize his or her own cash to exercise. Sometimes the needed cash is not available or, if available, then an immediate disposition of the stock must follow exercise to afford the process.

One alternative is a **stock appreciation rights (SAR)** plan. The plan allows employees to share in the appreciation of the stock without having to find the cash to fund this potential appreciation. The employee may or may not end up with the employer's stock. The employee may either take the appreciation of the stock in the form of cash compensation, which would be fully taxable as ordinary income,[33] or may buy the stock at the price granted by the employer and receive as compensation the difference between what the employee pays and the **fair value** of the stock. The example below reflects the "cashless" exercise of these rights.

Example 10: Stock Appreciation Rights

On January 2, 2001, corporation C grants to employee E SARs with respect to 1,000 shares of C's stock, which has a market value of $10 per share. The exercise period granted to E is five years. On January 2, 2004, when C's stock has a market value of $30 per share, E exercises the SARs by receiving from C $20,000. E recognizes ordinary compensation of $20,000 ($20 per share appreciation for 1,000 shares). Corporation C will take an ordinary compensation deduction of $20,000 in calendar year 2004.

J. TAX ASPECTS OF RESTRICTED STOCK

Another method of compensating employees is through the use of **restricted stock**. As the term indicates, the employer puts restrictions in place to retain key employees while rewarding them at the same time. The restrictions normally prevent the employees from selling or transferring the stock until some future date. Failure to observe the restrictions will result in forfeiture of the benefit.

As part of their incentive compensation process, employees may be granted an interest in shares of their employer's stock. The vesting in this stock may require the employee to work for a certain period of time to have full and complete access to the stock. If the employee terminates his or her employment before the restriction period, then the employee forfeits the stock.

The question then becomes, when is this benefit taxed to the employee? Because the employee does not have access to the stock until the restricted period lapses, there is no compensation income recognized at the employer's grant date. However, when the restriction period lapses and the employee vests in the stock, compensation is recognized.[34] The employee typically has the right to receive dividends paid with respect to the stock; the employer receives a compensation deduction with respect to any such dividends. The examples below illustrate these points.

Example 11: Restricted Stock Granted

On January 2, 1999, employee E receives as a bonus 1,000 shares of corporation C's stock. The stock has a fair market value of $10 per share. However, the employer requires E to remain employed for the next three (3) years or return the stock to C.

Tax Consequences:

Ordinary compensation to E in 1999:	None
Ordinary compensation deduction to C in 1999:	None

Example 12: Restriction Period Lapses

On January 3, 2002, the restriction period has lapsed and C's stock has a fair market value of $30 per share. Because the restrictions have lapsed, E is now vested in the stock and will recognize $30,000 of compensation.

Tax Consequences:

Ordinary compensation to E in 2002:	$30,000
Ordinary compensation deduction to C in 2002:	$30,000

If an employee is willing to gamble, the Internal Revenue Code provides the opportunity to convert some of the ordinary compensation such that E realized above into long-term capital gain income, and hence, more favorable tax treatment.

K. THE I.R.C. § 83(b) ELECTION

As was shown in Example 12 above, when the restrictions on the stock ended and E vested, ordinary compensation was recognized for the full value of the stock. I.R.C. § 83(b) allows E to make an election to report, as ordinary income, the value of the restricted stock received.

E will then have to pay tax at the regular rates on this income. This election then establishes the basis of the stock at that value. Three years from now, when the restrictions lapse, E can sell the stock and recognize a long-term capital gain for the appreciation in the stock above its base. This converts what would have been ordinary income attributable to the appreciation into long-term capital gain income.

Example 13: I.R.C. § 83(b) Election

Assume the same data as in Example 11, except E makes the I.R.C. § 83(b) election within 30 days after the stock transfer. E would recognize ordinary income of $10,000 as a result, and C would take a compensation deduction for the same amount. The basis of the stock would be established at $10,000. Assuming the stock price rises to $30 per share and E sells the stock, the appreciation would be capital gain income as opposed to ordinary income.

Tax Consequences:

Ordinary compensation to E in 1999:	$10,000
Ordinary compensation deduction to C in 1999:	$10,000
Stock basis established in 1999:	$10,000
Long-term capital gain recognized in 2002 when the stock is sold:*	$20,000

Long-term capital gain is determined by the selling price of $30,000 less stock basis of $10,000.

E, as would any taxpayer in this situation, is gambling that C's stock price will rise. By doing so, E is paying tax on the value of the stock on the grant date. If C's stock price declines, E would have already paid tax on a value that no longer exists. If this happens (or if E forfeits the stock due to an early departure from C), there would be no tax deduction allowed for the loss of value.

L. TAXATION AND THE IMMEDIATE OFFSET

The discussion thus far has focused on the tax consequences of exercising employee stock options and selling the underlying stock. On occasion, the titled spouse does not want to split the options but prefers to maintain ownership of all options. This may occur when the titled spouse believes the options have a greater current value than those derived from option pricing models, the titled spouse feels exercising and disposing of options will be negatively viewed by the employer, and possibly, the exercise of options of senior executives may be negatively viewed by the investors.

In these situations, the marital property settlement will call for the options of the titled spouse to be valued, and the value of the marital component of these options will be credited to the titled spouse. The contingent tax liability of the titled spouse must be taken into account when determining how much value is retained by the titled spouse.

As discussed, upon the exercise of a NQSO, the difference between the underlying share price at the time of exercise and the exercise price becomes part of the employee's gross income and is subject to tax at the prevailing ordinary income tax rates. Of course, one cannot know when the exercise will take place, what the tax rate will be at that time or the size of the gain. However, the timing of exercise and likely gain upon exercise both are factors that enter into the determination of the current value of the marital stock options using standard option pricing models. In other words, the current value of a NQSO at any point in time is based upon a gain occurring at the time of exercise. Stock option valuation models use explicit or probabilistic holding periods to determine value.

Given that the total option value is based upon a taxable gain occurring at a specific point in time, the tax impact of the future exercise must be deducted from the current value of the option. For example, assume that the current value of employee stock option using the BS-OPM is $20. Without showing the underlying math, the current option value of $20 is based upon the option exercised in five years with a taxable gain of $30.[35] Utilizing a 40% effective tax rate, the option holder will pay $7 in taxes upon exercise and net $18. To capture this future tax liability, the $20 current value must be tax impacted using a 40% tax rate resulting in a current after-tax value of $12. The relationship between current and future value is kept stable. The current pre-tax value of $20 is two-thirds of the expected future value of $30, and the current after-tax value of $12 is two-thirds of the expected future value of $18.

The result is that the present value of the likely future tax consequence will lower the current pre-tax value of the employee stock options. As previously stated, this is appropriate because the options will have only a current pre-tax value if one assumes a taxable event will occur in the future.

In most instances, employees who have incentive stock options also sell their stock upon exercise. In this situation, tax impacting the value of stock options at ordinary income tax rates is appropriate. The tax fact pattern is not as clear for the recipient of incentive stock options who does not dispose of the underlying stock after exercise. As previously discussed, both the length of time the option was held before exercise and when the underlying stock is sold will determine whether any resulting gain will result in capital gains treatment. Naturally, one cannot know at the time of the property settlement whether the titled spouse will or will not dispose of underlying stock supporting the value of the employee option. On balance, for the purpose of an immediate offset, the incentive stock options might be treated as if the underlying stock is sold at the time of exercise.

M. SUMMARY AND CONCLUSION

The Internal Revenue Code sets the tax treatment for the various approaches to employee compensation and its related impact on marital property settlements. Current tax rulings treat employee stock options similar to deferred compensation. This movement allows tax planning by both spouses to minimize the tax impact resulting from the exercise of employee stock options. As tax regulations are continually changing, parties should seek professional tax advice.

Notes

1. I.R.C. § 421 (2000).
2. I.R.C. § 421(a)(1) (2000).
3. I.R.C. § 421(a)(2) (2000).
4. I.R.C. § 83(a) (2000).
5. I.R.C. § 83(h) (2000).
6. I.R.C. § 83(a) (2000).
7. I.R.C. § 83(h) (2000).
8. I.R.C. § 83(e)(4) (2000).
9. I.R.C. § 83(a) (2000).
10. I.R.C. § 83(h) (2000).
11. I.R.C. § 83(e)(3) (2000).
12. I.R.C. § 83(a) (2000).
13. I.R.C. § 83(h) (2000).
14. S.E.C. Release No. 33-7646, 34-41109; File No. S7-2-98.
15. I.R.C. § 1041(a) (2000).

16. Rev. Rul. 2002-22, 2002-19, I.R.B. 849.
17. Rev. Rul. 2004-24, 2004-24, I.R.B. 1051.
18. I.R.C. § 3101(a) (2000).
19. I.R.C. § 3101(b)(6) (2000).
20. Economic Recovery Tax Act of 1981, Pub. L. No. 97-34, 95 Stat. 172 (1981).
21. I.R.C. § 421(a)(1) (2000).
22. I.R.C. § 421(a)(2) (2000).
23. I.R.C. § 422(b) (2000).
24. I.R.C. § 422(a) (2000).
25. I.R.C. § 421(b) (2000).
26. I.R.C. § 421(a)(1), (2) (2000).
27. I.R.C. § 56(b)(3) (2000).
28. I.R.C. § 422(a)(1) (2000).
29. I.R.C. § 421(b) (2000).
30. I.R.C. § 1041(a)(2) (2000).
31. I.R.C. § 424 (c)(4)(B) (2000).
32. I.R.S. Priv. Ltr. Rul. 200519011 (01-13-2005).
33. I.R.C. § 61(a)(1) (2000).
34. I.R.C. § 83(a) (2000).
35. In reality, the math required to estimate both the timing and the most likely share price at which the exercise will take place is extremely complicated. However, this does not detract from the conclusion that current value is based upon a taxable event taking place in the future.

Deferred Distribution v. Immediate Offset Approaches to Dividing Employee Stock Options*

4

After the court has determined the marital or community component of employee stock options, the next steps are to value the options and distribute or divide them. Similar to pensions, there are two major approaches to the distribution of options. The more prevalent method is not to value the options currently but to defer the distribution until the options vest and are exercisable. At that point, the net proceeds of the exercised options are divided on a percentage or equal basis between the parties. This method of distribution is referred to as the "if, as, and when approach" or the "deferred distribution" method. If, as, and when the options mature, vest, and are exercised, the proceeds are divided. The second, less-common approach is for the court to determine a present value for the options and award them entirely to the employee-spouse. Then, the court awards the nonemployee-spouse other assets of comparable value. This method typically is referred to as the "immediate offset" approach.

---

* The authors would like to thank Rachel Branson and Joleen Okun, clerks at Schnader Harrison Segal & Lewis LLP, and Meredith Brennan, an associate in the Family Law Department, who contributed to the writing of this chapter.

A. IMMEDIATE OFFSET APPROACH

Three state supreme courts have addressed the immediate offset approach. The first is a 1983 decision from Arkansas, *Richardson v. Richardson*.[1] In that case, the husband had options to purchase 3,000 shares of common stock of Murphy Oil Corporation at approximately $14 per share. At the time of the trial, the stock was trading at $22.50 per share. The options were exercisable at a profit of approximately $26,400. This figure was the difference between the option's cost and its current market price. The husband was awarded one-half of that amount. The Arkansas Supreme Court affirmed. The court's discussion of these issues is quite brief. The court stated that the options are a type of security that must be divided as marital property under Arkansas divorce law, and that the division awarded by the lower court was in compliance with the state's divorce statute. Two justices dissented on the theory that unexercised stock options are not property acquired by anyone because there is no guarantee that the option holder will make a profit.

In 1998, the Supreme Court of Connecticut addressed the issue in *Bornemann v. Bornemann*.[2] The court reached a similar conclusion to that reached by the Arkansas Supreme Court in *Richardson*. The *Bornemann* Court stressed the limited scope of review of a lower court's decision concerning stock options. Neither party introduced any expert testimony or information as to the value of the options. The court held that neither party now could complain on appeal that he or she was not satisfied with the lower court's valuation of the options when they presented such scanty evidence at trial.

> In this case, it was not a misapplication of the law for the trial court to have valued the asset on the basis of the scant evidence provided and to have distributed the asset on the basis of that valuation. The fact that neither party advocated a sophisticated method of valuation nor provided any particularly detailed or precise evidence of value in regard to the fourth and fifth flights of stock options did not preclude the trial court from equitably distributing those options.[3]

The trial court awarded the options to the wife.

Lastly, the Supreme Court of Nebraska addressed the property issue in *Davidson v. Davidson*.[4] In that case, the husband had received stock options from his employer, Union Pacific, since 1983. The trial court used the **Black-Scholes Options Price Model (BSOPM)** to value certain options because that method was used by the husband's accountants, by Union Pacific, and by the wife's expert witness. The lower court valued the entire marital estate at $5.3 million and awarded two-thirds to the husband and one-third to the wife.

The Nebraska Supreme Court's decision provides a much more detailed discussion of the valuation methods for stock options. This court recognized that other states have used the "deferred distribution" or "if, as, and when" method for valuing and distributing unexercised options. Under this approach, the wife would not receive her share of the marital estate comprised of unvested and vested, but unexercised, options until the options were eventually exercised. The court identified a constructive trust approach from New Jersey.[5] The court held that the lower court did not abuse its discretion by using the BSOPM because the husband's own accountant used that method on his financial statements, and Union Pacific used that method in its proxy statement. Using this valuation method, the lower court found that the total value of the husband's employee stock options and stock retention shares attributable to the marital estate was worth $5,655,974. This asset represented approximately 70% of the marital assets.

Six state Courts of Appeals have addressed the issue.[6] In a 1992 Michigan decision, *Everett v. Everett*,[7] the husband did not contest that his options were marital property but asserted that the Michigan trial court failed to consider several factors affecting the valuation of the options, including tax consequences. The court stated that it is required to accept the factual findings of the trial court unless those findings are "clearly erroneous." The court defined "clearly erroneous" as when the appellate court, considering all of the evidence, is "left with a definite and firm conviction that a mistake has been committed."[8] The appellate court cannot reverse the lower court if the lower court's view of the evidence is "plausible." This is a difficult standard to meet on appeal. The lower court's decision is given such deference because it had the opportunity to judge the credibility of the witnesses.

In this case, the trial court found that the husband's options were worth $102,445, which was the amount the wife testified to and alleged in her brief. However, she did not fully explain how she calculated this figure. In contrast, the husband presented expert testimony regarding a different method to value the options that resulted in a value of $50,861, approximately onehalf of wife's value. Subsequently, the husband testified that the options were worth $66,000, relying on his expert's formula. The court held that the trial court's view of the evidence was not plausible. The case was remanded to the lower court for a revaluation of the options. The court adopted the intrinsic value method to value the options. The date to use to determine the market price is for the lower court to decide. The court agreed with the husband that the trial court should take into consideration the tax consequences of the exercise of the options.

In the well-known 1998 case, *Wendt v. Wendt,*[9] the Superior Court of Connecticut, Stamford-Norwalk Judicial District at Stamford, made an exhaustive review of stock options and various methods used to determine their value, including the BSOPM. The court rejected all the available methods. The court held that the BSOPM is not appropriate for divorce cases even though it is generally accepted in financial circles. Ultimately, the court used the intrinsic value method which resulted in a lower value than the BSOPM. This method freezes the value based on the current stock price without any consideration of the real possibility that the stock price can increase in the future.

In 2000, the Court of Appeals of Louisiana, Fourth Circuit, addressed the use of the BSOPM in *Hansel v. Holyfield.*[10] The court characterized the issue as the wife asserting that the trial court erred in accepting the husband's expert's opinion rather than her expert's opinion. Her expert was an associate professor of finance from Loyola University. He used the BSOPM. In contrast, the husband's expert was an actuary. He used a present value/discount method. The trial court found this method more fairly and accurately established the present value of the options. The Louisiana Court of Appeals held that "the trial court was not *manifestly erroneous* or *clearly wrong* in accepting the opinions of Mr. Conefry (the husband's expert) over those of Mr. Christner (the wife's expert)."[11] (Emphasis added.) The Louisiana Appellate Court did not address the merits or flaws of the BSOPM.

In 2001, in *Henry v. Henry,*[12] the Court of Appeals of Indiana, Third District, remanded the case to the trial court with instructions to value the husband's unexercised stock options. In a footnote, the court states:

> We would suggest that the value of Michael's options be de-
> termined by the difference between the "striking price," which
> is typically the market price when the option was written, and
> the value of the stock on the day of the final hearing, times the
> total number of shares involved.[13]

This is the intrinsic value method rather than the BSOPM.

Finally, in 2002, the Court of Appeals of North Carolina dealt with these issues in *Fountain v. Fountain*.[14] In that case, the wife argued that the trial court erred by failing to apply the BSOPM, which she suggested should be the sole method for determining an option's value. As the BSOPM generally yields a much higher value than the intrinsic value method, it is not surprising that the nontitled spouses consistently argue for the application of that method. The BSOPM captures the potential future increase in the market price of the stock during the life of the option. The intrinsic value method does not pick up this potential added value. In any event, the Court of Appeals of North Carolina disagreed with the wife's position. Similar to the other states' scope of review on appeal, this court held that if it felt "the trial court reasonably approximated the net value of the [asset] . . . based on competent evidence and on a sound valuation method or methods, the valuation would not be disturbed."[15] The lower court had adopted the intrinsic value method. The court held that the trial court did not err in failing to adopt the BSOPM. The court cited an article from the *Equitable Distribution Journal* that the intrinsic value method is an accepted method along with the BSOPM.[16] The court also cited *Richardson v. Richardson, infra.*[17]

The lower court in *Fountain* awarded all of the options to the husband and awarded the wife a larger portion of the other assets. The decision was upheld on appeal. The wife argued that the trial court erred by not imposing a constructive trust over the options. The North Carolina Appellate Court rejected this argument. Interestingly, the lower court excluded the testimony of the wife's BSOPM experts. For some unstated reason, the wife did not list this evidentiary exclusion as a trial court error in her appeal or argue this point in her appellate brief. She did not raise the issue until oral argument before the North Carolina Court of Appeals. Not surprisingly, the court would not address this issue at that late stage of the appellate process. An issue not listed or identified by the appellant in his or her court filing and not raised in the appellate brief usually is considered waived by the time of oral argument.

To date, the only state to approve the use of the BSOPM in valuing stock options in a divorce case is Nebraska in *Davidson v. Davidson*.[18] However, the Nebraska court accepted the BSOPM because the parties and the corporation had used it. That is not the same as a court ruling that the method is reliable and accurate, endorsing its use in future cases. Given the limited scope of review of the appellate courts, the merits of the BSOPM versus the intrinsic value method have not been settled.

B. ARE OPTION PRICING MODELS OVERLY SPECULATIVE TO BE USED FOR EQUITABLE DISTRIBUTION?

In contrast to generally accepted accounting principles (GAAP) used in audited financial statements, SEC compensation disclosure, and the IRS estate tax valuation, courts have been reluctant to use option pricing models to determine the current value of employee stock options.

Although we agree with the decisions of several courts that it is impossible to know what a stock will be worth on any future date, it is not the case that the current value of a vested or unvested employee stock option cannot be measured with reasonable accuracy. For example, assume that an employee has Apple Computer employee stock options identical to the traded out-of-the-money options which are freely traded as shown in Table 4-1.

Table 4-1
Apple Computer, Inc. Traded Stock Options

Apple Computer (AAPL) Share Price Jan. 6, 2006: $76.30				
Exercise Price or Strike Price	Expiration Date	Cost or Market Value	Intrinsic Value	Time Value
$75.00	Feb. 17, 2006	$5.10	$1.30	$3.80
$75.00	Jan. 19, 2007	$15.10	$1.30	$13.80
$75.00	Jan. 18, 2008	$21.10	$1.30	$19.80
$85.00	Feb. 17, 2006	$1.50	$(8.70)	$10.20
$85.00	Jan. 19, 2007	$11.00	$(8.70)	$19.70
$85.00	Jan. 18, 2008	$19.00	$(8.70)	$27.70

The **out-of-the-money** options with a 2008 expiration date currently have a value of $19.00.[19] That is, the option exercise price exceeds the underlying share's share price. In this example, the option holder can purchase Apple Computer shares at $85 per share (exercise price) while the shares are trading at $76.30. As discussed in Chapter 2, out-of-the-money options often have a great deal of value, as do the out-of-the-money Apple Computer options. Does the lack of marketability inherent in the employee stock option make the option value so speculative that their value to the employee cannot be measured? Although the deferred distribution method provides many benefits, it also carries risk to the nontitled spouse, and the immediate off-set method should not necessarily be viewed as inferior to the deferred distribution method.

C. DEFERRED DISTRIBUTION APPROACH

The deferred distribution of stock options sets aside the options from the present distribution of marital or community property and instead distributes the proceeds from the options "if, as, and when received." The court retains jurisdiction over the matter to ascertain the value of the options on future dates when the options are actually exercised. This method eliminates the need to establish a current value because it does not require a present distribution of the assets. This method often is used when the current value of the stock options cannot be established or the options are subject to contingencies such that their value merely is speculative.

Several states have adopted this method of distributing stock options, although no state has determined that this approach is mandatory. Instead, these courts simply have held that the deferred distribution of such options is within the trial court's discretion. One case to fully examine the advantages and disadvantages of the deferred distribution method is *Fisher v. Fisher.*[20] In that case, the husband was awarded stock options as part of his compensation as an executive with the Harley-Davidson Corporation. After determining that the unvested stock options were marital property, the court turned to how the options should be distributed. Because the options in this case were nontransferable, the court found that the immediate distribution or transfer of the options would be impossible. Additionally, the court found that the immediate offset method was not feasible because the value of unvested stock options was "impermissibly speculative" and no value could be ascertained without unjustified assumptions. For these reasons, the BSOPM valuation method was specifically rejected. The court determined that the deferred distribution of the options was "unavoidable." It excluded the options from the present distribution and held the case open "for as long as necessary" to ascertain the value of the options when exercised, with the proceeds distributed equitably at that time. The *Fisher* court left open the possibility that options could be distributed immediately if the options were transferable, and at least one justice noted in a concurring opinion that the present value of stock options can be calculated using various methods, and that the immediate offset method should be used whenever possible.

Other states have adopted the deferred distribution method, including Colorado, Illinois, Maryland, Massachusetts, Missouri, New Hampshire, Virginia, and Wisconsin.[21]

There are several variations on the deferred distribution method that allow the nonemployee-spouse varying levels of control over the exercise of the options, as opposed to the "traditional" approach of the cases above, which generally allow the employee-spouse to determine if and when the options will be exercised. One such variation is the imposition of a constructive trust, whereby the stock options are held "in trust" by the employee-spouse for the nonemployee-spouse, and the court retains jurisdiction until the expiration of all of the options. Generally, the employee-spouse has a duty to notify the nonemployee-spouse when the options vest, and upon written instruction from the nonemployee-spouse, the employee-spouse must exercise such options on behalf of the nonemployee-spouse. The nonemployee-spouse also is generally responsible for the tax consequences to the employee-spouse for exercising the options.[22]

Another way to limit the employee-spouse's discretion in exercising the options is to specifically prescribe when the options must be exercised or to charge the employee-spouse a certain value, as courts in Alabama, Alaska, California, and Wisconsin have done.[23] For example, in *Broadribb v. Broadribb*,[24] the court found the husband's stock options to be marital property. The court directed that the options were to be exercised by a certain date, and that if the market price exceeded the option price during that period, the husband was required to exercise the options and divide the proceeds equally with his wife. In *In re Marriage of Harrison*,[25] after finding certain options to constitute marital property, the court ordered the husband to pay the wife her share of the proceeds of options when exercised, and if the husband chose not to exercise options, he was required to pay the wife her share of the gain that would have been realized had the options been exercised on the first date possible.

D. ADVANTAGES AND DISADVANTAGES

The deferred distribution method has several advantages. The primary advantage is that the proceeds are actual and not speculative. A second advantage is that the deferred distribution method does not require the employee-spouse to exercise the option against his or her will, or force him or her to liquidate other assets to "pay out" the other spouse. Yet another advantage is that this method assigns equally the benefits and risks of the exercise of the options. In contrast to the immediate offset method, which calculates a certain value for the options that may be greater or lesser than the value at the time of the actual exercise of the options, the deferred distribution method ensures that both spouses share the potential profit (or lack thereof) equally.

Of course, there are disadvantages to the deferred distribution method as well. The most often-cited disadvantage is that this method necessitates ongoing future legal proceedings between the parties and prevents finality and certainty in the litigation. The parties do not get a "clean break" from the marriage. The *Fisher*[26] court, for example, identified disadvantages involved where the employee-spouse is risk-oriented (and thereby holds on to the options with the hope that the value will increase, but the value actually decreases); is risk-averse (and thereby exercises the options on the first day they become available, instead of holding on to the options until they increase in value); or simply is vindictive (and thereby refuses to exercise the options at all to spite the nonemployee-spouse, even though he or she also foregoes any profit). The *Fisher* court's solution to these disadvantages was that the nonemployee-spouse could petition the court if he or she found evidence that the employee-spouse was not acting in good faith. Another solution is to use the constructive trust approach, which puts the decision to exercise or not to exercise the options in the hands of the nonemployee-spouse. One potential problem with constructive trusts is that it requires cooperation and communication between the parties, who very often do not wish to have a great deal of contact with each other. Another disadvantage of the deferred distribution is that, if the titled spouse changes jobs, existing options may be forfeited to the nontitled spouse unless replaced compensation can be explicitly identified.

The vast majority of divorce cases settle out of court, and thus the stock options usually are distributed pursuant to the terms of a written agreement. Assuming that the parties agree to distribute the options on a deferred distribution basis, it is essential that the attorney representing the nonemployee-spouse include protective language in any settlement agreement to safeguard that spouse's interest in and timely control over the exercise of the options at a reasonable market price, as well as his or her receipt of a fair share of the proceeds. See Appendix 4-A for sample protective language in a marital settlement agreement.

Most employee stock option plans forbid assignment of the rights created by the options granted. The rationale for this is that companies want to keep the options with the employees in the hope of keeping the employee with the company as well as providing a performance incentive. The practical effect is that, although a court may confer upon a nonemployee-spouse a right to the proceeds from a stock option, the options themselves are nontransferable. This tends to create agreement drafting problems for the parties and the court because the rights are to the option proceeds rather than the option itself. Agreements should take into consideration:

1. An explicit description of which options are marital and which are nonmarital;
2. A recitation of the terms for which the nontitled can compel the owner to exercise options after they have vested;
3. A precise calculation of the tax consequences arising from the transaction. For example, are taxes to be measured based upon their incremental impact or the average tax rate paid by the owner in the year the options are exercised;
4. A contingency if the titled spouse changes jobs and loses options;
5. An explicit discussion addressing whether the option value captured as property will or will not be treated as income for child support and alimony;
6. An explicit discussion addressing how **reload options** will be distributed if they exist; and
7. A plan for the options upon the death or long term disability of the titled spouse.

E. SUMMARY AND CONCLUSION

The deferred distribution method of dividing marital vested and unvested stock options has been preferred by courts. This method often is referred to as the "if, as, and when approach." The advantage of this approach is that it eliminates the need to estimate the current value of unvested stock options. Normally, a constructive trust is used to specify the process to be followed by the titled spouse to exercise newly vested options and distribute the proceeds to the nontitled spouse.

The immediate offset approach often is preferred by the titled spouse who believes the employee stock options may substantially grow in value. In addition, this approach creates a clean break between parties; whereas, the deferred distribution approach requires the parties to maintain a working relationship. The facts and circumstances in any given situation will, of course, determine which method makes the most sense.

Notes

1. 659 S.W.2d 510 (Ark. 1983).
2. 752 A.2d 978 (Conn. 1998).
3. *Id.* at 979.
4. 578 N.W.2d 848 (Neb. 1998).
5. *Id.* at 858 (citing Callahan v. Callahan, 361 A.2d 561 (1976)).
6. Michigan, Connecticut, Louisiana, Indiana, North Carolina and Texas.
7. 489 N.W.2d 111 (Mich. Ct. App. 1992).
8. *Id.* at 111.
9. 1998 Conn. Super. LEXIS 1023.
10. 779 So. 2d 939 (La. Ct. App. 2000).
11. *Id.* at 940.
12. 758 N.E.2d 991 (Ind. Ct. App. 2001).
13. *Id.* at 994.
14. 559 S.E.2d 25 (N.C. Ct. App. 2002).
15. *Id.*
16. *Id.* at 32.
17. *Id.* at 33.
18. 578 N.W.2d 848 (Neb. 1998).
19. A discussion of option valuation can be found in Chapter 2.
20. 769 A.2d 1165 (Pa. 2001).
21. *See In re* Marriage of Miller, 915 P.2d 1314 (Colo. 1996) (retaining jurisdiction to distribute the proceeds of the options when exercised and the restriction period relating to the options expired); *In re* Marriage of Frederick, 578 N.E.2d 612 (Ill. App. Ct. 1991) (retaining jurisdiction to distribute proceeds if, as and when options were exercised); Otley v. Otley, 810 A.2d 1 (Md. Ct. Spec. App. 2002) (approving deferred distribution method of options, but noting that the trial court has discretion to fashion an order to transfer options depending upon the type of restrictions on the options); Baccanti v. Morton, 752 N.E.2d 718 (Mass. 2001) (adopting deferred distribution method, noting that it is within trial court's discretion to determine in each case whether immediate offset or deferred distribution method should be used); *In re* Marriage of Smith, 682 S.W.2d 834 (Mo. Ct. App. 1984) ("distributing" one-half of the options to nonemployee-spouse where only employee-spouse was entitled to exercise options, but retaining jurisdiction over issues regarding the implementation and disposal of the options); *In the Matter of* Valence, 798 A.2d 35 (N.H. 2002) (distributing nonemployee's share of options to her if and when they vest); Dietz v. Dietz, 436 S.E.2d 463 (Va. Ct. App. 1993) (awarding nonemployee-spouse percentage of proceeds from the sale of stock options if and when exercised); *In re* Marriage of Chen, 416 N.W.2d 661 (Wis. Ct. App. 1987) (affirming deferred distribution of stock options, and noting method of distribution is within trial court's discretion).

22.　*See, e.g.,* Jensen v. Jensen, 824 So. 2d 315 (Fla. Dist. Ct. App. 2002) (approving deferred distribution approach to distribute unvested stock options, and imposing a constructive trust of the options upon the employee-spouse, which required him to advise the nonemployee-spouse when the options vest and to exercise the nonemployee-spouse's share of the options upon her direction); Callahan v. Callahan, 361 A.2d 561 (N.J. Super. Ch. Div. 1976) (holding that a constructive trust is appropriate in a case where the transfer of stock options is not profitable, possible or convenient); Banning v. Banning, No. 95 CA 79, 1996 Ohio App. LEXIS 2693 (Ohio Ct. App. June 28, 1996) (remanding case to trial court for determination of whether options were marital property and devising means of distributing such options, and specifically noting the method of a constructive trust); Boyd v. Boyd, 67 S.W.3d 398 (Tex. Ct. App. 2002) (awarding nonemployee-spouse one-half of the contingent value of employee-spouse's stock options, with employee-spouse acting as trustee for the nonemployee-spouse).

23.　956 P.2d 1222 (Alaska 1998).

24.　225 Cal. Rptr. 234 (Cal. Ct. App. 1986).

25.　*See, e.g., Chen,* 416 N.W.2d 661 (Wis. Ct. App. 1987) (awarding the wife an equal interest in the proceeds from the stock options if and when exercised, but directing that if the husband did not exercise the options within 18 months, the wife could elect to receive a payment in the amount of the present value of the option); Keff v. Keff, 757 So. 2d 450 (Ala. Civ. App. 2000) (awarding the wife 50% of the husband's stock options, but giving alternatives as to how the distribution was to be effected, including that the wife could elect to exercise her share of the options, or the husband could pay the wife the intrinsic value of the options).

26.　*Fisher,* 769 A.2d at 1165.

Appendix 4-A
Sample Language for the Division of Stock Options in a Property Settlement Agreement

THIS AGREEMENT entered into this day of _____, 20XX, between _____, residing at _____, (hereinafter referred to as HUSBAND) and ____, residing at _____, (hereinafter referred to WIFE); and

WHEREAS, the parties were married to each other on ____, and a Complaint for Divorce having been filed on ____; and

WHEREAS, pursuant to the terms of the Property Settlement Agreement dated, specifically Article Eight (8), the WIFE shall receive an interest by way of constructive trust of certain stock options as on Exhibit A; and

WHEREAS, the parties wish to establish a constructive trust for the benefit of the WIFE as it relates to various stock options granted by _____(hereinafter referred to as the "Company"); and

WHEREAS, the HUSBAND shall establish a constructive trust for the benefit of the WIFE for the stock options listed Exhibit A and no others;

NOW THEREFORE, in consideration of the mutual premises and covenants set forth herein, and in accordance with the Final Judgment of Divorce and Property Settlement Agreement, the parties agree as follows:

1.   The WIFE recognizes that her interest in the HUSBAND'S stock option grants and rights to restricted stock under this constructive trust are subject to the provisions of the plans (hereinafter referred to as the "Plans") under which they were granted.

2.   Federal securities law may prohibit the transfer, sale, or purchase of these securities on the basis of material, undisclosed information about the operations of the Company. Other legal restrictions and/or company restrictions relating to the transfer, sale, or purchase of these securities may also apply in some situations. Due to the nature of HUSBAND'S position at the Company, the HUSBAND may be required to obtain the internal authorization of the Company before exercising his stock options or transferring, purchasing, or selling Company stock. The WIFE recognizes and acknowledges that the HUSBAND may be prohibited from exercising stock options, purchasing, transferring, and/or selling Company stock due to federal securities laws and/or company restrictions. The WIFE recognizes and acknowledges that any such prohibitions or restrictions placed on the HUSBAND shall also apply to her rights and interests granted under this constructive trust.

3.　It is expressly understood that the WIFE shall hold the HUS-BAND harmless from any liability as a result of his failure to follow the WIFE'S instructions to exercise options, receive stock, or notify the WIFE that he has exercised options pursuant to paragraph 13 below, except in the case of his willful failure to adhere to her written notice.

4.　In the event the HUSBAND were to die prior to the exercise of his options or the vesting of his restricted stock, the WIFE would be entitled to her share of the benefit set forth on Exhibit A as a debt against the HUSBAND'S estate for the WIFE'S benefit, net of any taxes attributable to the WIFE'S interest.

5.　In the event the WIFE were to die prior to the exercise of her rights to the options or the vesting of her interest in the restricted stock as set forth on Exhibit A, the HUSBAND would be obligated to the WIFE'S estate for her interest, net of any taxes attributable to the WIFE'S interest.

6.　Subject to the above provisions and conditions, the WIFE shall provide to the HUSBAND written notice of her intention to exercise any of her vested stock options. The notice shall contain the chosen method of exercise and any cash payments or stock that is required as set forth below. The WIFE must accompany her notice with the funds or shares required under paragraphs 8, 10, or 11 below, and instructions as to the brokerage account to which she wishes any shares she will be receiving to be transferred. Upon receipt of said notice, the HUSBAND shall follow the WIFE'S instructions within seven (7) days or as soon as practical if the HUSBAND is unable to do so based upon such prohibitions or restrictions or his unavailability to do so.

7. If the WIFE chooses to exercise her options by a same-day sale, the HUSBAND shall exercise the options on her behalf within the time limits set forth above and provide the WIFE with the net proceeds from a same-day sale of the stock after deducting broker's fees and withholding _____ percent (xx%) on the taxable gain, attributable to such exercise and safe, with any adjustments to be made in accordance with paragraph 16 below.

8. The HUSBAND shall have a right of first refusal to retain the WIFE'S share of stock options by providing the WIFE with the equivalent cash, which she would have netted from the same-day exercise and sale of the stock after deducting broker's fees and withholding forty-five percent (45%) on the taxable gain, with any adjustments to be made in accordance with paragraph 16 below.

9. If the WIFE chooses to exercise an option by paying cash to purchase the related shares and hold same for her benefit, the WIFE

shall supply the HUSBAND with the funds necessary to purchase the shares as well as the income taxes attributable to the purchase, calculated at a rate of ___ percent (xx%) on the taxable gain, with any adjustments to be made in accordance with paragraph 16 below.

10. If the WIFE chooses to exercise an option using existing stock she owns to purchase the related shares, the WIFE shall supply the stock to the HUSBAND. The HUSBAND shall provide the WIFE with the net shares after deducting broker's fees and withholding ____ percent (xx%) on the taxable gain, with any adjustments to be made in accordance with paragraph 16 below.

11. The HUSBAND will use all reasonable efforts to notify the WIFE on the same day he has exercised any stock options subject to equitable distribution. The HUSBAND shall notify the WIFE in writing by either fax or email within two (2) business days of when he has exercised a stock option relating to any of the grant dates subject to equitable distribution.

12. If HUSBAND leaves the employment of ____ and, as a result, some or all stock options listed on Exhibit A are forfeited, then to the extent that HUSBAND is compensated by _____ or HUSBAND'S new employer, WIFE will receive net proceeds of such compensation. In the event HUSBAND receives deferred compensation related to the

forfeiture of stock options listed on Exhibit A, then the deferred compensation will be added to Exhibit A and be subject to this agreement.

13. In any year in which money is withheld by the HUSBAND or paid by the WIFE pursuant to this agreement and as soon as practicable after the HUSBAND files his income tax return for such year, the HUSBAND shall calculate the combined marginal tax rate ("Actual Rate") applicable to his income in such year. The Actual Rate shall be calculated by summing the highest of the Federal, State, local, and other tax rates applicable to his income for the year in question, after giving effect to the deductibility of State, local, and other taxes from his Federal taxable income for the year in question. Once calculated, the HUSBAND shall provide written notice to the WIFE of the Actual Rate. To the extent that there is a differential between the funds withheld by the HUSBAND or paid by the WIFE and the funds that would have been withheld or paid using the Actual Rate, either the HUSBAND or WIFE, as appropriate, shall make payment within ten (10) days of the WIFE'S receipt of the notice from the HUSBAND for any amounts due. By way of example, if the HUSBAND withholds 45%, and the Actual Rate is 40%, then the HUSBAND shall pay the WIFE an amount equal to the 5% differential. By way of further example, if the HUSBAND withholds 45%, and the Actual Rate is 48%,

then the WIFE shall pay the HUSBAND an amount equal to the 3% differential.

14. It is expressly understood that the HUSBAND shall have no obligation to produce or otherwise disclose his income tax returns for the year in question concerning the calculation in paragraph 12.

15. IN WITNESS WHEREOF, the parties have hereunto set their hands and seals the day and year first above written.

In the presence of:

_____

Stock Options as Income for Child Support and Alimony*

5

A. INTRODUCTION

Family courts across the country have divided or distributed stock options as an asset since 1984 when California did so in the seminal case, *In re Marriage of Hug.*[1] However, courts have been much slower to recognize options as a source of income available to pay child support. The first state to so hold was Colorado in *In re Campbell*[2] in 1995. Since that time, 12 additional states have held that stock options are income for child support purposes, and Arkansas is the only state that has held that stock options are not income for child support. Three state supreme courts have ruled definitively that stock options are income for child support purposes. Ten state appellate courts have found the same. A comprehensive chart of nationwide court decisions on stock options as income for child support purposes is included as Appendix 5-A. This chapter begins with a short list of key points matrimonial attorneys should consider when dealing with employee stock options and child support.

---

* The authors would like to thank Aisha Baruni and Joleen Okun, clerks at Schnader Harrison Segal & Lewis LLP, for their research support in writing this chapter.

B. WHEN ARE EMPLOYEE STOCK OPTIONS PART OF GROSS INCOME?

The purpose of child support is to maintain the standard of living to which the child is accustomed or to which the child would become accustom if the marriage had remained intact. It is true, however, that some states have limited the extent of child support where a formula outcome yields extraordinarily high child support results. Nevertheless, it is clear the prevailing view is that the child should not suffer financially because of the dissolution of the parent's marriage. This implies that, in decisions concerning executive stock options, the child's welfare takes precedence over the welfare of the titled parent.

States have not been consistent on when an employee stock option becomes income for child support. The general choices are: (1) at the time of grant; (2) at the time of vesting; and (3) at the time of exercise. A realized cash flow can only occur at the time one exercises the option, converting the option into underlying securities or cash. The following example illustrates these issues.

Example 1: When Employee Stock Options Become Income for Child Support

Titled spouse is granted 10,000 employee stock options of BFS Corporation on December 31, 1999. The options have a 10-year life with an exercise price of $50 per share. The options all vest on January 1, 2001.

Grant Date Values

At December 31, 1999 (**grant date**), BFS's share price was also $50 per share. At this date the options have an **intrinsic value** of zero as the share price equals the exercise price. However, BFS 1999 audited financial statement states that the fair value of these options on December 31, 1999, was $7. The fair value represents what the employee option could be sold for if it was marketable instrument. The fair value represents the value to the holder of the option.

Vesting Date Value

On January 1, 2001, the options vest. BFS's share price on January 1, 2001, is $49 per share. At this date the options have an intrinsic value of zero as the share price is less than the exercise price. It is also agreed that the fair value of the stock options is

$6.50 per option. Again, this value cannot be realized on January 1, 2001, but each option still has value because there is a good chance that the BFS stock will rise over $50 per share during the remaining nine-year life of the option. Of course, if BFS's share price were greater than $50 per share, the employee stock option would be **in-the-money** and have a positive intrinsic value, and its fair value would also be greater.

Value during Vesting Year
By year-end 2001 BFS's share price has risen to $60 per share. At year-end the intrinsic value has risen to $10 per option, and fair value of the employee stock options was estimated to be $15 per option.

Value at Exercise
The titled spouse exercises the option June 30, 2003, when the stock is at a value of $65 per share. Upon exercise the titled spouse sells BFS stock received through the option. The titled spouse receives $15 per option before consideration of taxes.

These pricing realities make the determination of income for child support a difficult process. The exercise of employee stock options as the trigger for the creation of income raises many issues because exercise can be delayed for many reasons. What if child support ends in 2002, and following the above example, the noncustodial titled spouse decides to exercise in 2003 to avoid increasing his or her gross income until child support ends? In the above situation, what if the titled spouse decides not to exercise his or her vested options because he or she believes that the option value will increase over the next several years? Is it appropriate that this rational economic decision result in no increase in gross income for child support?

Using the **vesting date** rather than the date of exercise to impute income for child support resolves some of these issues but unfortunately raises others. Employing the vesting date addresses the potential delay in exercise to after child support ends. In the above example, the employee stock options have a zero monetary value at vesting because the share price is less than the exercise price. Should this result in no change in gross income for purposes of child support?

By year-end BFS's share price increased to $60. Should courts use the average price of the stock during the calendar year of vesting to determine the intrinsic value of stock options? This would seem to deny the child the benefit that option holders enjoy—that is, the fair value of the stock options, which is always higher than the option's intrinsic value. Remember, at the date of vesting the option has a life of nine years during which the stock may increase in value. However, using **fair value** as income will redefine the concept of income for child support because the titled spouse cannot realize the $7 fair value of the option, as employee stock options cannot be sold. Should gross income include unrealizable value?

C. REVIEW OF COURT DECISIONS

With these issues in mind, courts have approached the inclusion and value of employee stock options for child support in two primary ways. Some courts have decided that income occurs at the time of exercise and others have decided that income occurs at vesting. There are no published decisions that income for child support occurs at the time employee stock options are granted.

Even though options do not directly represent cash income, states generally have held that vested stock options often meet the states' broad statutory definitions of "gross income."[3] Converting the asset value of employee stock options into income serves to minimize the economic consequences of divorce on children.[4] The New Hampshire Supreme Court in *In re Dolan*[5] expressed concern that, if exercised stock options were not counted as income for child support purposes, a parent would be able to avoid a child support obligation by choosing to be compensated in the form of stock options instead of a salary. Additionally, courts want children to enjoy a similar standard of living to that of their parents.[6] This concern, combined with the finding that stock options regularly are issued as a form of compensation, has led courts to count options as income when determining the child support obligations of the employee parent.[7]

In the California decision *Kerr v. Kerr*,[8] the Court of Appeals held that any realized income from stock options granted after divorce must be considered when computing the child support obligation of the employee-parent. Only the realized cash income from the exercised stock is income for child support purposes. As noted earlier, this method has the advantage of counting only "realized income," which avoids the need for a method to value the employee stock options. By counting realized income, a child support order will more closely reflect the resources immediately available for child support and the resources that could go to increase the parent's standard of living. As noted above, counting only exercised stock options, however, has several disadvantages. An employee-parent may choose to defer exercising the options until after his or her children have reached the age of majority, at which time the child support obligation terminates. A possible solution to this problem may be a court order requiring that the employee-parent exercise the option before the child reaches the age of majority.

The second method used to value stock options is to value them at the time of vesting or another appropriate date. This provides the court flexibility of choosing a time at which options will be valued for child support purposes. The courts determined a date, such as the date an option vests, and calculates the value of the options as its intrinsic value (the difference between the stock price and the exercise price on that date).

In *Murray v. Murray*,[9] an Ohio court focused on the first date a parent could exercise the options. This method determines the intrinsic value (share price less exercise price) on the first day on which the option could be exercised. The resulting profit is the value assigned to the option and the amount of income per share imputed to the employee-parent. The court notes that the option holder is responsible for transaction costs and taxes but is not clear on whether the deduction for taxes should be made before the court calculates the "profit" from an option. However, the option holder does not have to actually exercise the option under this approach.

One benefit of this method is an immediate increase in child support. Instead of waiting to see if an employee-parent chooses to exercise the options, the court ensures that the children are provided for, and parents are permitted to keep their investments as they see fit.[10] *Murray* recognized the concerns of parents regarding choice of date of valuation. It chooses the date the option can first be exercised in part to avoid the "games" of, for example, the obligor-parent choosing a date at which the option has a low value or the obligee-parent choosing the date with the highest possible value. By choosing the date the option is first exercisable, the court allows the parent to retain control over the options as an investment choice while recognizing the increased value of the assets over the period between grant and maturation. The court emphasizes the importance of the child support obligation as well as the nature of the options as a key form of compensation for the employee-parent. *Murray* addresses the economic and theoretical models used to value options on the open market and for other purposes, but finds that these models are not appropriate for child support cases.

Valuing an option at any specific date may result in an understatement of income. What if the option has an intrinsic value of $1 on the day of vesting and the share price of the underlying security continues to increase during the year? It must be reiterated that established financial research has been able to develop models that reasonably price nontraded options. Determining an estimate of the option's fair value would provide income for child support even for employee stock options that are out-of-the-money at the chosen measurement date. However, the imputed income will not be realizable at the measurement date, and most states do not count unrealizable income as part of gross income for child support calculations. This may place a burden on the nonguardian titled spouse.

Although the Arizona Appellate Court in *Robinson* followed the *Murray* method of valuation, it refused to adopt the intrinsic value method as the only valuation method involving stock options as income for child support. The court noted that it was important to maintain flexibility to meet the needs of families depending on the particular facts and circumstances of each case.

Not all courts that include unexercised stock options as income choose the vesting date for calculating present value. The Pennsylvania Superior Court in *Mackinley v. Messerschmidt*[11] assessed the value of the options as of the date used to determine all other sources of income for child support purposes. In this case, the court found this imputation of income a means of providing additional child support without requiring the employee-parent to exercise the options. The date chosen is different than that used in *Murray* and *Robinson*. This date has some advantages and disadvantages. The date of income calculation, for matured options, is later than the date the option first became exercisable. This may mean that a higher income will be imputed to the parent, but not necessarily depending on the performance of the stock market. If the income is higher, however, the result will be a higher amount of child support. The *Mackinley* court also is not clear as to whether taxes should be deducted when determining how much income an exercised option represents.

Because other sources of income are reduced by taxes in determining the amount subject to child support, the same should apply to options. The actual amount realized to the option holder is the profit less the taxes and transaction costs. To use gross profit without deducting these costs is unfair to the option holder.

Several courts have used a hybrid approach: a percentage model. In *Kerr*[12] and in *Robinson*,[13] California and Arizona courts, respectively, agreed that percentage awards are permissible. In *Kerr*, the trial court had applied the child support guidelines to the father's base income and then ordered that 40% of his bonuses and exercised stock option profits be added to the child support award. The Arizona court in *Robinson* did not actually use the percentage award method, but stated that the method was permissible.

Some courts have ruled only as to the use of exercised stock options as income and have not decided what method of valuation to use.[14] The New Hampshire Supreme Court in *Dolan*[15] and a Tennessee Appellate Court in *Stacey v. Stacey*[16] held that bonus and option income should be added to the husband's base salary to determine the child support obligation under the state's child support guidelines. Neither court addressed any of the other issues involved with the options as income or whether a deduction for taxes should be made. In *In re Cheriton*,[17] a California court counted the entire amount of the father's exercised stock options but noted that allowable deductions included taxes.

The issue of recurring versus nonrecurring income through the receipt of employee stock option income has been reviewed by several states. For example, a 1996 Ohio court held that options are not income for child support purposes in *Yost v. Uananue*.[18] The court held that the capital gain an employee-parent had received was not income for child support purposes because it was not recurring. The court found that the Ohio statutory definition of gross income excluded "nonrecurring income" and that the profit from the exercise of options qualified as nonrecurring income in a child support modification proceeding. In contrast, *Murray*,[19] a 1999 Ohio court decision, pointed out that, because the father received options annually, they were not inconsistent and therefore not excluded by the Ohio statutory definition of gross income. The court distinguished these factual circumstances from *Yost* due to the way that options were issued as part of the father's compensation package. In 2003, the Ohio Appellate Court in *Berthelot v. Berthelot*[20] followed *Murray*, but held that the court should also take the appreciation of the value of the stock into account. The *Berthelot* court noted that a parent should not benefit from the invest-ment without the child also benefiting. Other states, including New Hampshire, have noted that because their statutory definitions of in-come include gambling and lottery winnings and do not explicitly exclude options, options are to be included as income.[21] In New Hamp-shire, then, the issue is not whether the income is recurring.

D. THE CONSTRUCTIVE TRUST

A third method, which addresses the weaknesses of both measuring income upon exercise and measuring income at a specified date, has been proposed by Kristy Watson.[22] She has strongly encouraged the use of constructive trusts in counting stock options for child support purposes. However, no court has adopted this method yet.[23] Some courts have used constructive trusts in distributing stock options be-tween spouses in equitable distribution proceedings.[24] Watson argues that courts should impose a constructive trust on stock options, divid-ing the options between the parties in accordance with the percent-ages in the child support formula. The child would have an ownership interest in this percentage of the options. The nonemployee-parent would serve as trustee for those options.

Such a trust places a portion of the options into a trust to be man-aged by the custodial parent in the interest of the child. The trust re-lieves the titled spouse from having to make the decision of when to exercise an option and places that determination with the custodial parent. While recognizing that the custodial parent may well make poor exercise decisions, this methodology is quite appealing given the presumption that the welfare of the child is the primary concern of child support. Unfortunately, no court has yet applied this tool for child support purposes.

The advantage of the trust method is that it avoids the speculative nature of valuing unexercised options and removes the ability of an employee-parent to deny his or her child the financial benefit of the options. The primary disadvantage is the lack of experience courts have with this approach. A constructive trust, as Watson notes, recog-nizes the interest of the children as the most important consideration. It gives the trustee-parent the flexibility to determine when the options should be exercised for the benefit of the child. If the need is greater now, it can be exercised now. If the parent-trustee finds it is in the best interests of the child to delay exercise, that is also possible. For example, if the child is three years old, and private school is contemplated for the future, it might be wise to defer the exercise of the options until the private school tuition becomes due.

Employing the constructive trust methodology addresses the issue of valuing options for the purpose of income determination at a specific date. As discussed, this may lead to an understatement of income. Although the custodial parent may not have the financial sophistication of the titled spouse, the custodial spouse has the best interest of the child in mind, and potentially poor decisions simply are part of normal parenting. Alternatively, employing the option's intrinsic value rather than fair value to executive stock option valuation will almost certainly lead to a situation where the noncustodial-spouse earns more from his or her stock options than given up in child support. This is because the fair value of options, including executive stock options, will almost always exceed their intrinsic value. The trust also removes the issue of delaying the exercise until the child support ends if the deferred distribution method is employed.

The tension between the short-term and long-term benefits of options as an asset or as income available for child support might be addressed through the constructive trust as discussed above. No court has yet required an employee-parent to immediately exercise his or her options to provide for child support, but it remains a possibility. The forced exercise of options may be a shortsighted solution to dealing with the role of options in supporting children. An option holder usually chooses to refrain from exercising his or her options to see if the stock price increases over time. This increase in value could benefit the minor children as well as the employee-parent. Forcing the exercise at today's prices may result in lost financial resources for the family unit. Similarly, immediately imputing a value to unexercised options may disadvantage children of an employee-parent who earns a greater profit when he or she actually exercises the options. Imputing income, however, is preferable to forcing the exercise of the option because it preserves the potential for a parent to earn a higher profit, which may ultimately benefit the children depending on how the additional profit is used.

Some commentators have criticized the use of options as income. Karns and Hunt[25] focus on the potential to lose money, particularly through federal income tax liability. This focus, however, is centered not on the well-being of the children, which should be the primary focus of family courts facing child support disputes, but on the ability of an employee-spouse to maximize his or her own income for personal gain and favorable tax treatment. If the well-being of children is the primary interest of state courts, should children be penalized for the poor business judgment of their parents in determining when to exercise options? If the nonemployee-parent argues that the employee-parent should have exercised an option earlier to take advantage of a better market, should the court adjust the income level attributed to that parent? Is the court in any better position to evaluate the best time to exercise stock options? After all, judges are not in the business of making investment decisions for litigants. At first, this idea appears to contradict the very nature of stock options and the unpredictable fluctuations of the stock market. However, as expressed by the *Murray* and *Robinson* courts, it is a proper for the court to prevent an employee-parent from skirting his or her support obligation by deferring the exercise of his or her options. To safeguard the interests of children, a court may have no choice but to determine whether the employee-parent exercised reasonable business judgment at the time he or she chose to exercise the option. The evidence needed for a court to make this assessment includes an analysis of the parent's intentions as well as testimony concerning the performance of the stock market to determine whether the decision to exercise was reasonable.

Judges likely will be extremely hesitant to substitute or impose their judgment as to the best time to exercise options. As a practical matter, by the time a case reaches the courtroom, the stock price may have already peaked. By the time of the trial, the price may be lower than when the moving party initially filed for support modification. Is it fair or reasonable to impose a price or value on the option that is impossible for the titled spouse to achieve by the time the court hears the case? Given stock market volatility, it is unfair to expect a spouse to know precisely when the stock price has peaked and to exercise the option at that exact moment. Even the best financial advisor cannot pinpoint or forecast that price. On the other hand, what if the stock price drops to the point that the option is "under water" by the time of the support trial? The titled spouse could have resisted exercising the option to defeat the other spouse's support claim. It is unfair to the nontitled spouse to assign a zero value to the stock option.

E. USING EMPLOYEE STOCK OPTIONS AS PROPERTY AND INCOME

The inclusion of stock options as income for child support purposes may be in the best interests of the children, but there are many practical problems that can arise. One of the most controversial issues is the "double-dip" problem, i.e., counting stock options as both an asset and as income. Many courts that have been critical of the inclusion of stock options as income fear that options will be distributed first as an asset in equitable distribution and then counted a second time as income for support purposes. This is financially detrimental and unfair to the employee-parent.[26] In some cases, this problem does not arise because the options are acquired after divorce and are not subject to equitable distribution. Other courts find that they are income, not an asset, and consequently should not be equitably distributed.

Several states have refused to classify the same options as both an asset and income. In *Denley v. Denley*,[27] a Connecticut court held that stock options already equitably distributed could not be considered income for the purpose of modifying a child support order. The court noted that the "mere exchange of an asset awarded as property in a dissolution decree, for cash, the liquid form of the asset, does not transform the property into income."[28] To date, courts have not addressed the issue of whether a large portfolio of options compromised of pre-separation and post-separation options could be apportioned partially as a marital asset and partially as income.

In *Colangelo v. Sebela*,[29] the trial court allocated 50% of vested options to the nontitled spouse and 100% of the unvested options as part of the property division. Child support was based upon 20% of net monthly income of the noncustodial parent and 20% of any bonus/commissions received net of taxes. The issue was whether the exercise of the unvested stock options within the property agreement should count toward the calculation of net income for child support. The trial court excluded option proceeds using the logic that the capital gain of an investment property used in a marital settlement would not be income for purposes of child support. On appeal, the court stated that, ". . . even though the unrealized stock options were allocated to the parties as marital property, the realized stock distribution met the definition of 'income' for purposes of determining child support. . . ."[30] The Appeals Court noted that, in Illinois, child support looks to income from all sources and that in previous decisions income from retirement assets divided as part of property settlements are included as income for the calculation of child support.

In summary, child support generally is viewed as provided by a spouse's gross cash income. When an employee stock option vests, it becomes an asset that can be converted into pre-tax cash income upon exercise. The immediate cash value of an employee stock option (its liquidation value at a point in time) at the time of vesting may be zero or positive. However, the intrinsic value is almost always less than the option's fair value.

F. ALIMONY AND SPOUSAL MAINTENANCE

Five states have addressed stock options as income available to pay spousal maintenance or post-divorce alimony. Unlike child support, where states almost uniformly hold options are income, the court decisions on spousal maintenance and alimony go both ways.

When determining whether stock options are income for maintenance or alimony, courts have dealt primarily with options, which have already been divided pursuant to equitable distribution or community property division as part of the divorce proceedings. No court has approved the characterization of options as income for the purpose of alimony if they have already been characterized as an asset and equitably distributed.[31] In *Hamlin v. Hamlin*,[32] the Minnesota Court of Appeals held that because the stock options in question were divided in a property settlement, they were not additional income for alimony purposes. In *Seither v. Seither*,[33] a Florida court recognized stock options as income for alimony purposes. The trial court had not characterized the options as an asset; consequently, they were not equitably distributed. The appellate court found no abuse of discretion in finding these stock options to be calculated as income available to the husband to pay spousal and child support.

Alimony is decided based on different factors and criteria than child support. It is determined in conjunction with property distribution. Therefore, the double-dip problem should be treated more seriously in this context. In equitable distribution and alimony cases, the former spouse is the beneficiary of the court award. To treat options as an asset and as income would benefit that spouse twice. This differs from child support, however, where children are the beneficiaries of the support award. On the other hand, the definition of income for alimony purposes often is the same as for child support. There is no reason, in principal, why this income should be included for one form of support and not for the other. With only five states having addressed the issue, there is no clear trend yet across the country.

A chart of nationwide court decisions addressing stock options as income for alimony or spousal maintenance appears in Appendix 5-B.

G. PROPERTY SETTLEMENT AGREEMENTS

A common provision in a property settlement agreement (PSA) is that child support (or alimony) is modifiable upon a substantial increase in the payor's income. If the payor-spouse is awarded stock options after the PSA is signed, are such options to be included as income? What if the language of the parties' PSA provides for a child support increase only if the payor receives a bonus? Should the grant of employee stock options be considered a bonus? For example, what if employee stock options are granted in lieu of a cash bonus, but vest after child support ends. Of course, divorce counsel can include specific language in the PSA that address these issues. What if the PSA already has been signed and does not address post-divorce options? In that case, the underlying facts of the option must be examined to see if the option is a form of income or bonus.

A New Jersey court addressed these issues in *Heller-Loren v. Apuzzio*[34] and ruled that post-divorce options are not income under the terms of a PSA. The PSA provided that the parties would each pay a pro-rata share of the children's expenses based on their respective "gross earned income," which was defined as "all gross wages, commissions, salaries, bonuses, and income from businesses."[35] The court held that because the parties did not include options in the definition of income in their PSA, they did not intend to consider options in determining the amount of child support. The pre-divorce options were addressed in the PSA and distributed to the husband. Yet, the PSA was silent about post-divorce options. The options in question were awarded two years after the PSA. The court's decision was based on the principles of contract interpretation. In effect, the New Jersey Appellate Court adopted the lower court's ruling that this was an "intentional omission." The fact that each party agreed to waive any claim to property acquired in the future by the other party in the PSA was also a factor in the appellate court's decision. The drafting of divorce settlements must be abundantly clear with respect to how stock options are to be handled.

For example, in the section of the settlement agreement reprinted below, the titled spouse felt he was able to defer additional support payments by choosing not to exercise his vested options until 2006. The nontitled spouse argued for the 15% pursuant to the PSA.

> **The parties' respective obligations as to the support and maintenance . . . The wife will also receive an additional fifteen percent (15%) of any net bonus received by the husband . . . same for child support through 2005. Net bonus shall be defined as gross bonus monies received by the husband less taxes. . . .**

A review of documents established that the employer granted employee stock options in lieu of cash bonuses. This resulted in the parties agreeing to place 10% of the granted options in a trust for the children.

H. OTHER SPECIAL CIRCUMSTANCES

The situation in which a parent is terminated from employment and must exercise all existing options or lose them raises other concerns. Assume the termination occurs on September 1, 2005. The parties separate on January 1, 2006, but the wife does not file for support until April 1, 2006. The options are reported as taxable income for 2005 only. Usually, child support is based on the parent's current income. The husband's current income in 2006 arguably does not include the 2005 option income. If the state's child support guidelines use average income over the previous six months, the options in this example would not count as income for child support purposes. If the guidelines use the previous 12 months of income, then the options would count. If the options do not count as income, then they should be counted as an asset subject to equitable distribution or community property division.

Divorce counsel must consider whether the client is better off counting options as an asset subject to property division or as income subject to support. The nonemployee-spouse probably would be better off characterizing the options as an asset to receive 50% or more of the asset on a tax-free basis in equitable distribution states. If the option is treated as income, the nonemployee-spouse likely is to receive less than 50% as alimony or child support. Moreover, the alimony portion of the award is taxable to the nonemployee-spouse. Even worse, the alimony portion often terminates upon the nonemployee-spouse's cohabitation or remarriage. These termination events do not apply to options divided as property. On the other hand, if the marital estate is worth millions of dollars, the nontitled spouse typically may be awarded less than 50% of the assets. In that case, the percentage awarded to the nonemployee-spouse may be no different whether it is awarded in the form of property distribution or support. If the nonemployee-spouse has no desire to cohabit or remarry, those distinguishing factors may also not apply. The nontitled spouse and his or her counsel must carefully weigh the advantages and disadvantages of characterizing options as an asset or as income to determine which approach is better under the particular facts and circumstances of the case.

Finally, divorce counsel should consider the nonmarital portion or component of a stock option. If the court applies a time rule as discussed in Chapter 1 and finds that a portion of the option is nonmarital, then that portion is not divided as property. However, that portion still is available as a source of income to pay alimony or child support. In this way, the nontitled spouse can receive a portion of the nonmarital component of the option through a support claim.

I. SUMMARY AND CONCLUSION

How child support is impacted by the granting and subsequent exercise of employee stock options is a topic with more questions than answers. Vested employee stock options represent value to the option holder but may have no realizable value at the date of vesting. The timing of the exercise of employee stock options may provide the titled spouse the ability to deny a child support. Courts generally have considered vested options income upon exercise (when they are converted into gross cash income) or upon vesting (when the ability to convert the option into income becomes possible). These differing methodologies may yield significantly different outcomes for child support. The constructive trust is one way to manage these issues; however, there are no published decisions at this time using this device. State courts have taken different positions on whether employee stock options can be used for both property settlement agreements and for child support. The list of cases in Appendices 5-A and 5-B will assist attorneys in developing strategies in their determination of how employee stock options impact child support.

Notes

1. 201 Cal. Rptr. 676 (1984).
2. 905 P.2d 19 (Colo. 1995).
3. *See, e.g.*, West Virginia v. Baker, 557 S.E.2d 267 (W.Va. 2001).
4. *Id.* at 267.
5. *In re* Dolan, 786 A.2d 820, 823 (N.H. 2001).
6. *Id.* at 823.
7. *Id.*; *see also Murray, infra* note 9.
8. 91 Cal. Rptr. 2d 374 (Cal. Ct. App. 1999); *see also In re* Campbell, 905 P.2d 19 (Colo. 1995) (understanding unexercised options as potential income).
9. 716 N.E.2d 288 (Ohio App. 1999).
10. *See, e.g., In re* Robinson, 35 P.3d 89 (Ariz. Ct. App. 2001).
11. 814 A.2d 680 (Pa. Super. 2002).
12. *Kerr*, 91 Cal. Rptr. 2d at 381.
13. *Robinson*, 35 P.3d at 89.
14. *See, e.g., Baker*, 557 S.E.2d at 267.
15. *Dolan*, 786 A.2d at 824.
16. 1999 Tenn. App. Lexis 668 (Oct. 6, 1999).
17. 111 Cal Rptr. 2d 755 (Cal. Ct. App. 2001).
18. 671 N.E.2d 1374 (Ohio Ct. App. 1996).
19. *Murray*, 716 N.E.2d at 288.
20. 796 N.E.2d 541 (Ohio App. 2003).
21. *See, e.g., Dolan*, 786 A.2d at 820.
22. *See* Kristy Watson, Note, *Acting in the Best Interests of the Child: A solution to the problem of characterizing stock options as income*, 69 FORDHAM L. REV. 1523, 1541 (2001).
23. *Id.* at 1541.
24. *Id. See also* Callahan v. Callahan, 361 A.2d 561 (N.J. Super. Ct. Ch. Div. 1976).
25. *See, e.g.*, Jack E. Karns & Jerry G. Hunt, *Should Unexercised Stock Options be Considered "Gross Income" Under State Law for Purposes of Calculating Monthly Child Support Payments?*, 33 CREIGHTON L. REV. 235, 240 (2000).
26. *See, e.g.*, Denley v. Denley, 661 A.2d 628, 631 (Conn. App. Ct. 1995); Kapfer v. Kapfer, 419 S.E.2d 464, 467 (W.Va. 1992); Hamlin v. Hamlin, 1993 WL 469139 (Minn. Ct. App. 1993).

27. 661 A.2d 628 (Conn. App. Ct. 1995).
28. *Id.* at 631.
29. 355 Ill. App. 3d 383 (2005).
30. *Id.* at 579.
31. *See, e.g., Denley*, 661 A.2d at 628.
32. 1993 WL 469139 (Minn. Ct. App. 1993).
33. 779 So. 2d 331 (Fla. Dist. Ct. App. 1999).
34. 853 A.2d 997 (N.J. Super. Ct. 2004).
35. *Id.*

Appendix 5-A
Nationwide Court Decisions on Stock Options as Income for Child Support Purposes

State	Case Name	Citation	Comment
Arizona	*In re Marriage of Robinson*	35 P.3d 89 (Ariz. Ct. App. 2001)	Stock option is income for child support; court uses value at time exercisable but declines to adopt this method for use in all future cases.
Arkansas	*Southerland v. Southerland*	58 S.W.3d 867 (Ark. App. 2001)	Finding lump sum payment for nonvested options in corporate takeover was not income for child support.
California	*In re Marriage of Cheriton*	111 Cal. Rptr. 2d 755 (Cal. Ct. App. 2001)	Exercised options are income for child support.
	Kerr v. Kerr	91 Cal. Rptr. 2d 374 (Cal. Ct. App. 1999)	Where former husband had history of receiving stock options from employment throughout marriage, trial court was justified in finding that his alimony obligation included a percentage of his receipt of stock options in the future.
Colorado	*In re Marriage of Campbell*	905 P.2d 19 (Colo. App.1995)	Gross income includes income from "any source," including options, for child support.
Delaware	*Kenton v. Kenton*	571 A.2d 778 (Del. 1990)	Profits from exercise of options count as income for child support.

State	Case Name	Citation	Comment
Florida	*Seither v. Seither*	779 So. 2d 331 (Fl. Dist. Ct. App. 1999)	Stock options may be considered income for child support.
Illinois	*In re Marriage of Colaneglo*	822 N.E.2d 571 (2005 Ill. App. Ct.)	Marital property can also be used for child support.
New Jersey	*Heller-Loren v. Apuzzio*	853 A.2d 997 (N.J. Super. Ct. 2004)	Exercised stock options are income for child support purposes. Whether the income is recurring is also an issue under NJ law.
New Hampshire	*In re Dolan*	786 A.2d 820 (N.H. 2001)	Exercised stock options are included in income for child support.
Ohio	*Berthelot v. Berthelot*	796 N.E.2d 541 (Ohio Ct. App. 2003)	Exercised and unexercised vested options are income for child support.
	Murray v. Murray	716 N.E.2d 288 (Ohio Ct. App. 1999)	Unexercised stock options are income for child support.
	Yost v. Unanue	671 N.E.2d 1374 (Ohio Ct. App. 1996)	Exercised options are nonrecurring income and not gross income for child support.
Pennsylvania	*Mackinley v.*	814 A.2d 680 (Pa. Super. Ct. 2002)	Unexercised stock options are income available for child support.

State	Case Name	Citation	Comment
Tennessee	*Stacey v. Stacey*	1999 Tenn. App. Lexis 668 (Tenn. Ct. App. Oct. 6, 1999)	Stock options are income for child support; bonuses and options averaged and added to husband's base salary.
Texas	*In re Interest of C.J.*	2001 WL 493701 (Tex. App. 2001) (unpublished)	Income from stock options should be included in computing monthly net income for child support.
	Haselbarth v. Haselbarth	1998 Texas App. Lexis 320 (Tex. Ct. App. Jan. 15, 1998)	Amount contributed monthly to employer's stock option plan is income for child support.
Virginia	*Forsythe v. Forsythe*	1996 WL 1065613 (Va. Cir. Ct. 1996)	Stock options exercised or paid out are "clearly" gross income.
Washington	*Ayyah v. Rashid*	38 P.3d 1033 (Wash. Ct. App. 2002)	Proceeds from exercised options should be included in income calculation for child support.
	Nolan v. Nolan	1999 WL 639409 (Wash. Ct. App. Aug. 23, 1999)	Upholds child support award above guidelines because father had been granted stock options previously and would likely receive them again.
West Virginia	*West Virginia v. Baker*	557 S.E.2d 267 (W.Va. 2001)	Holding income realized through the exercise of a stock option is within the definition of "gross income" in the relevant statutory section.

Appendix 5-B
Nationwide Court Decisions on Stock Options as Income for Alimony and Spousal Maintenance

State	Case Name	Citation	Comment
California	*Kerr v. Kerr*	91 Cal. Rptr. 2d 374 (Cal. Ct. App. 1999)	Stock options husband received in future as part of compensation package were income for maintenance and child support purposes.
Connecticut	*DeAnda v. DeAnda*	2000 WL 1765450 (Conn. Super. 2000) (unpublished opinion)	Income from the exercise of stock options is not income for alimony purposes.
	Denley v. Denley	661 A.2d 628 (Conn. App. Ct. 1995)	Stock options not income for alimony.
	Burns v. Burns	677 A.2d 971 (Conn. App. Ct. 1996)	Court upheld trial court's award of periodic alimony payments, including percentage from future stock option bonuses. No specification when options valued.
	Sims v. Sims	593 A.2d 161 (Conn. App. Ct. 1991)	Stock options not income because exercised only once and there were no expectation of receiving future options.
Florida	*Seither v. Seither*	779 So. 2d 331 (Fl. Dist. Ct. App. 1999)	Stock options considered income for alimony purposes.

State	Case Name	Citation	Comment
Iowa	*Moore v. Moore*	2000 WL 564165 (Iowa Ct. App. May 10, 2000)	Percentage award of future options granted to wife.
Minnesota	*Hamlin v. Hamlin*	1993 WL 469139 (Minn. App. 1993) (unpublished opinion)	Because stock options were divided in the property settlement, the options were not available as income for spousal maintenance.

Index